Paul on Homosexuality

Paul on Homosexuality

Michael Wood

Tubi Publishing, LLC

Paul on Homosexuality

Copyright © 2011 by Michael Wood

Scripture quotations marked (NASB) are taken from the New American Standard Bible®,
Copyright © 1960, 1962, 1963, 1968, 1971, 1972, 1973, 1975, 1977, 1995 by The Lockman Foundation
Used by permission. (www.Lockman.org)

Scripture quotations marked (NIV) are taken from the Holy Bible, New International Version®, NIV®.
Copyright © 1973, 1978, 1984, 2010 by Biblica, Inc.™
Used by permission of Zondervan. All rights reserved worldwide.
www.zondervan.com

ISBN: 978-1-936565-12-2 (pbk)

ISBN: 978-1-936565-13-9 (hrc)

ISBN: 978-1-936565-14-6 (ebk)

Printed in the United States of America

Contents

Foreword

The Roman Empire was Paul's world, but the *lingua franca* of that world was Greek. From Europe to Egypt to the borders of Persia and India, most of the world's business was transacted in Greek. The populations of the eastern Empire had learned Greek centuries before, in the wake of Alexander's conquests, while in the West, even in Italy and Rome itself, Greek was the common tongue of merchants, slaves, entertainers, artists, musicians, and all sorts of public servants involved with administering the Empire. Greek continued, as always, to be the language of philosophy, of science, and of higher education in general.

As a member of the Jewish diaspora in far-flung Cilicia, Paul grew up with Greek as his native language, while the proper tongue of his cultural heritage, the Hebrew language, was restricted to the synagogue. It was in Greek that Paul thought, argued, and preached, whether he was dealing with Gentiles or fellow Jews. Even his Bible was written in Greek, translated centuries before from the original Hebrew by seventy rabbinical scholars in Alexandria, Egypt (it is from the Latin word for "seventy" that we call that Bible the "Septuagint").

Paul's letters, which make up most of the New Testament, show that his Greek was of a highly literate character. He was able to convey both subtlety and profundity in the "common" (*koinē*) conversational Greek of his day. His speech in those letters to his beloved flock could be as elevated as Plato's—but, like Plato's, it was still conversation. The challenge for the modern scholar is to be alert to the special characteristics of Paul's prose, and to reproduce them in a contemporary language that brings out the Apostle's spirit in all its clarity and grace.

Michael Wood has gone the extra mile in being faithful to Paul's Greek. He has transcended the facile interpretations and mistranslations of conventional Bibles, from King James onward, and broken through to Paul's original and consistent meaning. Dismissing the meaningless (but traditional) translation of "righteousness" for *dikaiosune* and *dikaiomata*, he goes to their Greek origins, and specifically to the Septuagint, where he finds their true meanings rooted in ideas of loving kindness, fairness, and justice. This discovery points directly, of course, to the ideas expressed in the Sermon on the Mount, and confirms Paul's orientation toward the one Commandment that is the whole of the Law: Love your neighbor as yourself.

Still being faithful to the Greek, Michael has been guided by the tenth-century Byzantine scholar, Photius, to find a solution to the Great Paradox in the first three chapters of Romans — the contradictory statements (1) that only those who follow the Law shall be saved, and (2) that no one who follows the Law shall be saved. Michael Wood reveals to the public a well-kept secret, namely that the apostle Paul, like the rest of his contemporaries, divided the commands of the Jewish law into two groups demarcated by Leviticus 19:18—"Love your neighbor as yourself." All commandments based on loving your neighbor were "Justices of the Torah" (*dikaiomata tou nomou*). Those not based on Leviticus 19:18 were "Jobs of the Torah" (*erga tou nomou*), commandments between man and God. It was the Justices that constituted the "whole" Law for Jesus and Paul; it was the Justices, summed up in "Love your neighbor as yourself," that superseded all the "Jobs" of the Torah. To follow the Justices is to be saved; to follow the Jobs is to be lost. Understanding this division of the Torah removes the contradiction once and for all.

This is a remarkable discovery, because it solves a colossal paradox that has remained unsolved for 2000 years. It not only shows that Paul is perfectly consistent; it also makes Paul consistent with Jesus. Beyond that, it makes Christianity finally consistent with itself. The whole Law is loving kindness—loving kindness toward everyone of every race, gender and sexual orientation. Again applying a rigorous standard to the translation of Paul's Greek, Michael Wood shows, time and again, that the words traditionally mistranslated as "homosexual," "effeminate," "impure," and so forth, are really targeting selfish, unloving, unjust activity and have nothing to do with sexual orientation. As for sexual activity in general, Paul, while not condoning, does not condemn unless an injustice is involved (like seducing another's wife).

It has been a great privilege for me to work with Michael on this book, because the book cannot help but effect a positive change in Christian attitudes. For the first time in two millennia, Christians can see that Jesus and Paul had the same message for us: that we owe each other, and God, nothing but love for each other, for "Love doesn't think evil, doesn't enjoy injustice, and rejoices with the truth" (1 Corinthians 13:5-6).

William Berg, Ph.D.

October 2011

Preface

Homosexuality is one of the most hotly debated religious issues of our time. The debate is consuming a lot of time, energy, and money. It is even ripping longstanding denominations apart. Yet, there is only one unequivocal reference to homosexuality in the Greek New Testament, and that is in Romans 1. Ironically, this reference to homosexuality is contained within a Biblical passage that has befuddled theologians for the last 2,000 years, since the very birth of the Christian faith.

One of today's great Biblical scholars, Dr. Richard N. Longenecker, describes the issue this way: "The interpretation of Romans 1:18-3:20 has been notoriously difficult for almost every commentator.... Earlier interpreters such as Origen, Jerome, Augustine, and Erasmus wrestled with this issue, and it continues to plague commentators today." Why is Romans 1:18-3:20 such a mystery? Dr. Longenecker explains, "No one being able to be declared righteous by observing the law (Romans 3:20) is clear, [yet] there are four texts in Romans 2 that seem to espouse a theology of salvation by works or by obedience to the Mosaic Law."

Over the last two millennia, various theories have been offered to reconcile Romans 1:18-3:20 (the only passage that contains an unequivocal reference to homosexuality). Yet no one, literally no one, had been able to explain Paul's message in a way that accounts for every sentence in the passage. Every theory proposed has contradicted at least one part of the passage. For example, Romans 2:13 basically says that only those who keep the entire Law will be vindicated before God. John Calvin, the founder of Baptist doctrine, hypothesized that Paul meant that no one can be found who has kept the entire Law. The problem is that, in the very next sentence (Romans 2:14), Paul gives an example of those who keep the entire Law and are justified before God for doing so. Calvin joined the long list of commentators who were unable to reconcile every sentence of this mysterious passage.

As a cryptographer, I love unsolvable puzzles. I have been blessed in my lifetime to have solved a number of previously unsolved puzzles in a variety of fields: in cryptography (by designing one of the only unbreakable codes in existence today); in data communications (by building an artificial intelligence system that accurately deduces how an entire world-wide network is physically wired together); in neurology (by making a system that monitors the real-time activity of the nervous system branch that is responsible for all recuperative and healing functions); etc. Each of these successes was based upon first resolving a previously unsolved issue. Each issue had befuddled those in the respective fields for a very long time. So it was only natural that I applied the same discipline to the Romans 1:18-3:20 issue that I was so deeply familiar with.

Having grown up in an evangelical Christian household as a PK (Preacher's Kid), I literally fell in love with the Bible. I even memorized Paul's letter to the Romans word for word. I knew the Romans 1:18-3:20 paradox quite intimately. A few years ago, I had the good fortune of totally and completely solving the paradox. I had discovered a single explanation that accounts for every sentence in the passage. This was the first time in 2,000 years that this had been accomplished. I published the solution in *The Jesus Secret*. The discovery served as the basis of my later work, *Breaking the Romans Code*.

The historic resolution of the paradox has tremendous implications. No longer are multiple "theologies" acceptable. There is only one solution to the paradox. Any theology that doesn't resolve the paradox isn't a viable alternative; it is simply wrong. The resolution of the paradox inherently proves what Paul's message was in Romans 1:18-3:20. The 2000-year-old question has been answered. The theological game is over.

While I revealed the full answer to the paradox in *The Jesus Secret* and *Breaking the Romans Code*, I didn't spend a great amount of time dealing with the implications of this discovery as it relates to homosexuality, an integral part of the passage. The present work, *Paul on Homosexuality*, has been written to rectify this. The solution to the 2000-year-old mystery incidentally reveals the historical Paul's view of homosexual relationships. Quite surprisingly, the resolution of the paradox proves that traditional Christianity's misunderstanding of Romans 1:18-3:20 resulted in a misunderstanding of Paul's view on homosexual relationships. Now, with the definitive solution to the paradox, this is about to change.

To those who want to know what the historical Paul actually taught about homosexual relationships: Welcome.

Michael Wood

October 2011

Acknowledgments

To Dr. William Berg for whom I am grateful beyond that which words can express.

To Esteban Serrano and Osvaldo Jerez whose constant support and encouragement has made this work possible.

To Jaime Alberto Castano and Juan David Yanes whose willingness to critique so many revisions helped fine tune many important distinctions.

Chapter 1

Bipolar Disorder

On May 10, 2011, the Presbyterian Church (USA) became the fourth major Protestant denomination to accept the ordination of gay and lesbian clergy.[1] To conservative Presbyterians, this move signaled that their Church had completely abandoned Biblical principles. The Bible seemed to have no authoritative weight anymore. So conservatives are now leaving the denomination in droves. They are separating over what seem to be irreconcilable differences.

But are the differences truly irreconcilable? When all is said and done, the primary obstacle to unity comes down to a difference in opinions regarding one man: the apostle Paul. From the conservative perspective, Paul unequivocally declared that no homosexual shall enter the kingdom of God. If liberals can reject clear, unambiguous scriptures, then the Bible must not matter to them at all.

Reverend Wheeler explains the conservative perspective:

St. Paul makes an explicit statement condemning homosexual practice in his letter to the Romans:

God gave them over in the sinful desires of their hearts to sexual impurity for the degrading of their bodies with one another. They exchanged the truth of God for a lie, and worshiped and served created things rather than the Creator—who is forever praised. Amen. Because of this, God gave them over to shameful lusts. Even their women exchanged natural relations for unnatural

---

1   New York Times, May 10, 2011.

> ones. In the same way the men also abandoned natural relations with women and were inflamed with lust for one another. Men committed indecent acts with other men, and received in themselves the due penalty for their perversion.—*Romans 1:24-27*

There are lists of disobedient types of people, including homosexuals, that are condemned in St. Paul's other letters, specifically I Corinthians and I Timothy:

> Do you not know that the unrighteous will not inherit the kingdom of God? Do not be deceived; neither fornicators, nor idolaters, nor adulterers, nor effeminate, nor homosexuals (also trans.: sexual perverts), nor thieves, nor {the} covetous, nor drunkards, nor revilers, nor swindlers, will inherit the kingdom of God.—*1 Corinthians 6:9-10*

> The law is not laid down for the just but for the lawless and disobedient, for the ungodly and sinners, for the unholy and profane, for murderers of fathers and murderers of mothers, for manslayers, immoral persons, sodomites [homosexuals], kidnappers, liars, perjurers, and whatever else is contrary to sound doctrine.—*1 Timothy 1:9-10*

There is no scriptural reference that can be found to support the purported morality of homosexuality. So, the testimony of Scripture is irrefutable in its prohibition of homosexuality and emphatic in its condemnation of those who practice it. There is no honest way around this issue, as inconvenient as it may be to people of the present day who revel in the dark pleasures of homosexual intercourse, and enable others to do the same.[2]—Reverend Wheeler (Pastor of Holy Cross Church)

From the conservative perspective, Paul wrote *three times* that homosexuality is a despicable abomination which absolutely prohibits a person from entering the kingdom of God. With such clear, repeated condemnation, what more needs to be said?

So how do liberals respond to this? Herbert W. Chilstrom explains:

> To use the Bible to condemn homosexual persons and committed faithful same-sex relationships is, we believe, to bear false witness against the Bible.

> We also want to assure you that we are against all sin whether it is

---

2   "The Abomination of Homosexuality in the Episcopal Church" by Fr. Lawrence B. "Chip" Wheeler, January 9, 2010

homosexual, heterosexual, or nonsexual. We understand sin in light of Christ-centered texts such as this passage from the apostle Paul:

> Owe no one anything, except to love one another; for the one who loves another has fulfilled the law. The commandments, "You shall not commit adultery; you shall not murder; you shall not steal; you shall not covet"; and any other commandment, are summed up in this word, "Love your neighbor as yourself." Love does no wrong to a neighbor; therefore, love is the fulfilling of the law. (Romans 13:8-10)

We understand that written word of Scripture in light of Jesus who is the living Word. Christ, who is Lord of all, is also Lord of the Bible.[3]—Herbert W. Chilstrom (the first ELCA bishop)

Here is the dilemma. Conservatives believe that Paul wrote *three times* that homosexuals cannot enter the kingdom of God, while liberals believe that Paul wrote *three times* that loving our neighbors as ourselves (bearing the burdens of others) is the sum total of God's moral and ethical requirements:

> Don't owe anything to anyone beyond loving one another because he who loves others has fulfilled the Law, because "don't commit adultery," "don't murder," "don't steal," "don't covet," and if there is any other commandment it is summed up in these words: "You shall love your neighbor as yourself."[4]— Paul

* * *

> The whole Law is fulfilled in one precept: "Love your neighbor as yourself."[5]—Paul

* * *

> Bear one another's burdens and thereby fulfill the Law of Christ.[6]—Paul

From the liberal perspective, marrying someone of the same sex doesn't violate "Love your neighbor as yourself." A married gay couple can bear the burdens of others and thereby fulfill the entirety of Jesus' requirements. Therefore, it's impossible for homosexuality to

---

3   *Sexual Fulfillment for Single and Married, Straight and Gay, Young and Old*, by Herbert W. Chilstrom, Lowell O. Erdahl, pp. 122-123, Augsburg Books, 2001
4   Romans 13:8-10
5   Galatians 5:13-14 as translated by Dr. William Berg
6   Galatians 6:2 as translated by Dr. William Berg

be against God's Law.

Atheists, meanwhile, simply shake their heads. They can't understand why liberals and conservatives fight over a man whom the Bible portrays as suffering from a split personality disorder. To them, Paul is a self-contradictory loon who touts loving your neighbor as the entire Law on the one hand, while condemning homosexuality on the other. They view the Bible as one of the most self-contradictory books on the planet, and it boggles their minds that anyone would ever consider taking it seriously.

So did Paul really teach that loving your neighbor as yourself is the entire Law, only to take it back when it came to homosexuals? Did he really go back and forth *three times*? Was he really that bipolar?

As an internationally acclaimed cryptographer, I was intrigued by the puzzle. It seemed impossible that any sane man would have taken two opposing views of his God's requirements. It seemed that there must have been something else going on that got lost in modern translation. Therefore, after consulting with Dr. William Berg (who holds a PhD in Classical Studies from Princeton University), I was able to finally put the historical pieces together. It turns out that there is a single, unified reason why Paul wrote what he did about loving our neighbor and sexuality. In fact, it turns out that Paul's teachings are two sides of the same coin.

So who was the apostle Paul? Did he believe that Jesus' Golden Rule is the entirety of Christian obligation, as the liberals assert? Or did he believe that the entirety of Moses' moral code (the one that prohibits homosexuality) is still in force as the conservatives assert? Setting aside religiously motivated theological arguments, who was the *historical* Paul? What did the actual man of history believe?

Chapter 2
Beautiful Ideal

The Jews of Paul's day embraced a beautiful concept they called "practicing *dikaiosune*." This concept involved the practice of making the needs of others equal to your own:

> And for all those who **practice *dikaiosune*** from out of your possessions give your alms... Give of your bread to the hungry one, and from your clothing to the naked ones; make an almsgiving from everything that you have more than enough for you.[7]

Practicing *dikaiosune* involved sharing your extras with those in need. Jesus, Paul's master, spoke about this in his famous Sermon on the Mount:

> Beware of **practicing your *dikaiosune*** before men to be noticed by them; otherwise you have no reward with your Father who is in heaven. **So when you give to the poor**, do not sound a trumpet before you, as the hypocrites do in the synagogues and in the streets, so that they may be honored by men; truly I say to you, they have their reward in full. But **when you give to the poor**, do not let your left hand know what your right hand is doing.[8]

Jesus used the phrase "practicing *dikaiosune*" in accordance with the traditional Jewish meaning: sharing your extras with the poor.

Flavius Josephus, another contemporary of Paul, wrote that John the Baptist commanded his converts to "practice *dikaiosune* towards one another."[9] How exactly did John the Baptist explain this

---
7   Tobit 4:6-7, 16
8   Matthew 6:1-3 NASB [with *dikaiosune* untranslated]
9   Antiquities 18.5.2

concept?

> John the Baptist said to them, "The man who has two shirts is to share with him who has none, and he who has food is to do the same."[10]

Three historical Jewish sources (including Jesus himself) document that "practicing *dikaiosune*" meant "sharing your extras with those in need." In other words, in Jewish culture, "practicing *dikaiosune*" meant practicing altruism. With this in mind, let's take a look at what John, one of Jesus' disciples, wrote to his converts:

> In this the children of God and the children of the devil are made known: **anyone who does not practice *dikaiosune* is not of God.**[11]

Well, that's pretty direct, isn't it? The historical meaning of the phrase tells us precisely what John wrote:

> In this the children of God and the children of the devil are made known: **anyone who does not practice altruism is not of God.**[12]

If you are an avid reader of the Bible and wonder how you missed John's very clear message, don't worry. It's not your fault. It's something that got lost in translation. Chances are, your Bible says something like this:

> By this the children of God and the children of the devil are obvious: anyone who does not practice **righteousness** is not of God[13]

Now let me ask you this: Out of every one hundred people who read the translation above, how many will know what the original Greek text actually said? None of them will. They can't. The translation teaches something different from what John wrote. And here's the problem. No conventional Bible actually teaches what John wrote. They all teach something different. Hundreds of millions of people are being taught something different than what Jesus' disciple actually wrote.

---

10   Luke 3:11
11   1 John 3:10
12   1 John 3:10
13   1 John 3:10 NASB

What does this have to do with Paul? *Dikaiosune* was one of Paul's favorite words. In fact, the central message of his letters is framed around this Greek term. Modern Bibles translate his letters as discussions about "righteousness." But was the historical Paul hyper-focused on righteousness or altruism? Was he hyper-focused on morality or ethics? Who was the historical Paul?

Chapter 3

What's Love Got to do with it?

The apostle Paul grew up in the ancient city of Tarsus. In his city, many Jews were more familiar with Greek than with Hebrew. Therefore, they used a Greek translation of their scriptures. That Greek translation, created two hundred years before Paul's time, is known as the Septuagint:

> An awareness of the role of the Septuagint in Paul's religious outlook is crucial for understanding the letters....
>
> Much of the language shaping Paul's identity and outlook came from the Greek translation of the Hebrew scriptures that we call the Septuagint....
>
> As an important feature of the Judaism of Paul's day,[14] the Septuagint was the Bible not just of the elite scholars but of the common people. While retaining some of its Jewish flavor, the Septuagint, composed in the ordinary Greek of the day, was fully intelligible even to the illiterate person who heard it read or cited in synagogue settings. Not only was Paul a "Septuagint-Jew," as Adolf Deissmann called him nearly a century ago, but the same was also the case for most synagogue Jews in Tarsus.[15]—Calvin J. Roetzel (Arnold Lowe Professor of Religious Studies and award winning researcher on the apostle Paul).

Paul grew up immersed in the Septuagint. An understanding of Septuagint terminology is absolutely critical to comprehending him. His use of the term *dikaiosune* is a prime example of this. That Greek word was used in the Septuagint, in a variety of passages, to translate

---

14   "Paul's Diaspora Judaism" in the text
15   *The Letters of Paul: Conversations in Context* by Calvin J. Roetzel, p. 20, Westminster John Knox Press, 2009

the Hebrew word for "loving kindness."

- The Septuagint used *dikaiosune* to translate the Hebrew word for "loving kindness" in Genesis 19:19, 20:13, 24:27, according to Charles H. Talbert (Distinguished Professor of Religion at Baylor University). [16]

- The Septuagint contains instances where "living in *dikaiosune*" means to "practice love of one's neighbor," according to Benedikt Otzen (Professor of Old Testament Exegesis at the University of Aarhus). [17]

- The Septuagint translation introduced "the additional element of love" into *dikaiosune*, according to Willem A. VanGemeren (Professor of Old Testament and Semitic Languages at Trinity Evangelical Divinity School).[18]

Scholars, far and wide, recognize that the Septuagint often used *dikaiosune* to express "loving kindness." Isaiah 63:7 is one such example:

> According to all that the LORD has granted us,
> And the great goodness toward the house of Israel,
> Which He has granted them according to His compassion
> And according to the **abundance of His loving kindnesses**.[19]

In the Greek Septuagint, the phrase "abundance of his loving kindnesses" is translated as "abundance of his *dikaiosune*."

It is essential to understand that Paul's Bible often used *dikaiosune* to express "loving kindness" (altruism). Why is this so important? Consider what Paul wrote to his Roman converts:

> offer your members to God as instruments of *dikaiosune*.[20]

16   *Reading the Sermon on the Mount: Character Formation and Decision Making in Matthew 5-7*, by Charles H. Talbert, PhD, Univ of South Carolina Press, 2004.
17   *Tobit and Judith* by Benedikt Otzen, p. 32, Continuum International Publishing Group, 2002
18   *Interpreting the Prophetic Word: An Introduction to the Prophetic Literature* by Willem VanGemeren, p. 364, Zondervan, 1996
19   Isaiah 63:7b NASB
20   Romans 6:13

We now have a dilemma. Did Paul command his converts to use the members of their body as instruments of "righteousness" (as conventional translations say)? Or did Paul command his converts to use the members of their body as instruments of "loving kindness" (in accordance with the expanded Septuagint usage)? What did the historical Paul actually teach?

Chapter 4
Body Parts

To the first-century man on the street, *dikaiosune* meant "justice and fairness." However, the Septuagint expanded its range to include "loving kindness"[21] (i.e. treating others altruistically).

The Greek Septuagint served as the Christian Old Testament for the first five hundred years of the Faith. The original Christian recipients of Paul's letters read from the Greek Septuagint. They were intimately familiar with both street Greek and Septuagint Greek. For example, when they read Romans 6:13 in their native language, they understood:

> And don't present the members of your body to sin as instruments of injustice, unfairness, and unkindness. But present yourselves to God as alive from the dead, and present your members as instruments of justice, fairness, and altruism unto God.[22]

Unfortunately, modern Bibles translate this passage quite differently. They portray Paul as commanding his converts not to use

---

21 For examples of *dikaiosune*, compare the Hebrew to LXX for Genesis 19:19; 20:13; 21:23; 24:27, Exodus 34:7;15:13, Psalms 106:3-4 (*dikaiosune* and *krisis* as synonyms for *eudokia* [benevolence]), 112:9, Isaiah 63:7; see also Matthew 6:1 where "practicing *dikaiosune*" means "practicing altruism" (practicing making the needs of others equal to your own). For the verbal imperative *dikaiosate*, see Isaiah 1:17 LXX. For the adjective *dikaios* see Psalms 37:21 LXX. For the plural masculine noun *dikaioi*, see Matthew 9:13 (used as a synonym for Hebrew chesed [loving kindness]), and Matthew 25:37, where the *dikaioi* are those who feed the hungry, shelter the homeless, and clothe the naked, i.e. those who treat others altruistically.
22 Romans 6:13

the members of their body as instruments of moral 'unrighteousness.' The modern translations portray the passage as if it were abounding in sexual innuendo:

> Do not go on presenting the members of your body to sin as instruments of unrighteousness; but present yourselves to God as those alive from the dead, and your members as instruments of righteousness to God.[23]

So was the apostle Paul concerned about the Romans using their body parts for unrighteousness or the unkind treatment of others? What was the historical Paul concerned about here? Three chapters earlier, Paul gave a sample list of the type of misuse of body parts that he was referring to:

> [Chapter Three]
>
> **There isn't anyone showing kindness**, not even one.
> **Their throat** is an open tomb.
> They deceive with **their tongues**.
> The poison of snakes is under **their lips**;
> **Whose mouth** is filled with curses and bitterness.
> **Their feet** are eager to shed blood.[24]

In Romans 3, Paul wrote about people who once used their throats, tongues, lips, mouths, and feet as instruments for the unjust, unfair, and unkind treatment of others. He wrote that these folks who misused their body parts were lacking in kindness. Then in chapter six, he commanded his converts not to be like these people. One passage seamlessly parallels and blends with the other.

> [Chapter Six]
>
> And don't present the members of your body to sin as instruments of injustice, unfairness, and unkindness. But present yourselves to God as alive from the dead, and present your members as instruments of justice, fairness, and altruism unto God.[25]

Conventional Bibles have ripped apart this seamless fluidity by their insertion of moral "righteousness" into chapter six. Chapter six has been disconnected from chapter three. The warm and inspiring message of loving kindness and altruism has become lost in translation.

23   Romans 6:13 NASB
24   Romans 3:12-15
25   Romans 6:13

The historical Paul has become lost in translation as well.

Chapter 5

Terms of Enslavement

The very heart and soul of Paul's writings have been ripped out of modern translations. Take Galatians 5:13, for example:

> Through love serve one another.[26]

Conventional Bibles claim that Paul told his converts to "serve one another" in love. "Serve one another" sounds like the type of service that a waitress might give to her customers. But the underlying Greek word is discussing a much stronger form of service. It is, quite specifically, demanding *enslavement*.[27, 28]

> The NAB translation actually masks the full force of Paul's language, which literally calls upon them "to be *slaves* (imperative *douleuete*)" of one another through love.—Brendan Byrne (Melbourne College of Divinity, Department of Biblical Studies)[29]

Paul used the Greek word *douleuete* to tell his converts that they were "*enslaved* to one another through love."

---

26   Galatians 5:13b NASB

27   *Slave of Christ: A New Testament Metaphor for Total Devotion to Christ* by Murray J. Harris, p. 80, InterVarsity Press, 2001

28   *Paul in the Greco-Roman world: A Handbook* by J. Paul Sampley, p. 617, Continuum International Publishing Group, 2003

29   *Galatians and Romans* by Brendan Byrne, p. 43, Liturgical Press, 2010

- Paul commands the Galatians to "'enslave' themselves to one another 'through love,'" teaches Frank Thielman (Professor of Divinity, Samford University).[30]

- "Paul exhorts the Galatians to enslave themselves to one another through love," teaches Walter J. Harrelson (Religion Professor Emeritus at Vanderbilt University).[31]

- Galatians 5:13 says, "Through love be enslaved to one another," teaches Frank J. Matera (Professor of New Testament, Catholic University of America).[32]

Evangelical, mainstream Protestant and Catholic professors alike teach their students that Paul wrote about *enslavement* in Galatians 5:13. Yet none of the Bibles handed out in churches tell their readers about this. The average man in the pew is never told what Biblical scholars know.

Why do modern conventional translations weaken Paul's words? When Paul's words are translated correctly, we learn that the historical Paul told his converts that they are *enslaved because of the Law*:

> You are enslaved to one another through love **because** the entire Law is fulfilled in one statement, in the precept, "Love your neighbor as yourself."

Enslavement *because of the Law* is enslavement *to the Law*. Conventional theology rejects the concept of enslavement to any law. Therefore, modern translators expunge the concept from their versions of the Bible. They rewrite the Biblical text to appeal to the modern consumer. Who's going to buy a Bible that says something different from what their Church teaches? The actual words of the historical Paul have been sacrificed in the process.

But the concept of enslavement to love is the heart and soul of Paul's writings. In fact, it is the heart and soul of *both* Galatians and

---

30   *The Law and the New Testament: The Question of Continuity* by Frank Thielman, p. 19, Crossroad Pub., 1999
31   *The New Interpreter's Study Bible: New Revised Standard Version with the Apocrypha* by Walter J. Harrelson, p. 2,087, Abingdon Press, 2003
32   *Galatians* by Frank J. Matera, Daniel J. Harrington, p. 193, Liturgical Press, 1992

Romans.

It is in Galatians that Paul wrote:

You are enslaved to one another through love.[33]

And in Romans, he wrote:

Having been emancipated from sin you became enslaved to loving kindness [*dikaiosune*].

As a reminder: the altruistic loving of others is one of the first-century meanings of *dikaiosune*. Yet modern Bibles unanimously translate Paul's words in Romans as enslavement to "righteousness":

Having been freed from sin, you became slaves of righteousness.[34]

The religious rewrite of Paul makes him appear to be an ultra-conservative who is overly fixated on moral righteousness. The historical Paul, however, was an extremely different person. He was hyper-focused on getting his converts to treat other people justly, fairly, and altruistically.

It's important to understand *why* Paul was so focused on loving others. It's important to understand his motivation. It's important to know what was driving him. Paul insisted that his converts love one another *because the entire Law is fulfilled in the precept, "Love your neighbor as yourself."*

You are enslaved to one another through love **because the entire Law is fulfilled in one statement, in the precept, "Love your neighbor as yourself."**[35]—Galatians

* * *

Having been emancipated from sin you became enslaved to loving kindness…. he who loves others has fulfilled the Law **because "don't commit adultery," "don't murder," "don't steal," "don't covet," and if there is any other commandment it is summed up in these words: "You shall love your neighbor as yourself."**[36]—Romans

33   Galatians 5:13
34   Romans 6:18 NASB
35   Galatians 5:13-14
36   Romans 6:18, 13:8b-9

It bears repeating: enslavement *because of the Law* is enslavement *to the Law.* The historical Paul believed that his converts must enslave themselves to a Law that is fulfilled by "loving our neighbors as ourselves."

But now, we have another dilemma. For Paul also commanded his followers not to be enslaved to the Torah (Moses' Law). In fact, he wrote that anyone who follows the Torah is under a curse:

For those who keep the Torah's Jobs are under a curse[37]

If Paul didn't want his converts to follow the Torah, then which law did he demand his converts to be enslaved to? Which law is entirely fulfilled in the precept, "Love your neighbor as yourself"?

37   Galatians 3:10. See chapter 9, "Justices and Jobs," for a full discussion on the Torah's Jobs.

Chapter 6
New Age

At the turn of the first century, the ancient Jewish nation was expecting the arrival of a prophesied leader called the Messianic King. They believed that he would establish a new era called "the Age of the Messianic King."

One school of Jewish thought expected the coming Messianic King to replace the Torah with a Law of his own:

> The Torah that a person learns in this age is trifling compared to the Law of the Messianic King.[38]

Such Jews considered the Torah to be insignificant compared to the Law of the Messianic King. They considered the Torah to have only been put into place until his arrival:

> The world is to exist six thousand years. In the first two thousand years there was chaos. Then two thousand years the Torah will flourish. And then the next two thousand years is the Age of the Messianic King.[39]

While the adherents of this line of thought were in the minority, their viewpoint was widely known and widely recognized. Their school of thought is represented in early rabbinic literature, including the Babylonian Talmud:

---

38 *Koheles Rabah* 11:8
39 *T Sanhedrin* 97a—According to the citation, this teaching comes from *Baraithas* (the Oral Law which extended back to the time of Paul).

18

According to some, the Torah was expected to cease in the messianic age; others held that the Messiah would perfect the law by giving it a new interpretation or that he would promulgate a new Torah.

Though the dominant thrust of the rabbinic tradition was that Torah would continue in and through the messianic age, that it was eternally valid, there are also many who thought there would be modifications, that some teachings would cease to be applicable, that others would acquire new relevance, that the sacrificial system and festivals would cease, that ceremonial distinctions between "clean" and "unclean" would no longer hold. Thus, a rabbinic tradition which both affirmed the continuance of the law in the messianic age and also recognized some form of cessation and/or modification forms the backdrop for Paul's experience and new understanding. The messianic age had dawned. The Torah could no longer be seen as before.—Manfred T. Brauch (Retired Professor of Biblical Theology and past President of Palmer Theological Seminary of Eastern University).[40]

* * *

There was also a tradition in Judaism that in the age of the Messiah a new Torah would be given, a perfect "Torah of the Messiah" (= "law of Christ" in Gal 6:2).—David Arthur DeSilva (Dr. DeSilva is a specialist in the fields of Second Temple Judaism, the social and cultural environment of the first-century Greco-Roman world.)[41]

So which school of thought did Paul belong to? Did he believe that the Torah was put into place only until the arrival of the Messianic King? Did he believe that the Torah was superseded by the Law of the Messianic King?

But to Abraham were spoken the promises, and "to his seed;" it doesn't say "and to his seeds," referring to a lot of people, but referring only to one: **"to your seed," that is the Messianic King…. So what is the Torah? It was something put in to take care of transgressions until the seed [the Messianic King] should come.**[42]

* * *

I myself was not under the Torah… but under the Law of the Messianic King.[43]

---

40   *Hard Sayings of Paul* by Manfred T. Brauch, pp. 58-59, InterVarsity Press, 1989
41   *An Introduction to the New Testament: Contexts, Methods & Ministry Formation* by David Arthur DeSilva, p. 482, InterVarsity Press, 2004
42   Galatians 3:16,19 as translated by Dr. William Berg
43   1 Corinthians 9:20-21 as translated by Dr. William Berg

In Galatians, Paul explained that the Torah was put into place only until the Messianic King arrived. In 1 Corinthians, he explained that he was not under the Torah, but under the Law of the Messianic King instead. Paul belonged to the school of thought that expected the Torah to be superseded by the Law of the Messianic King. This is a critical distinction.

For Christians, Jesus of Nazareth was the Christ—the prophesied Messianic King. They believed that the Messianic King's arrival *necessitated* a change in law:

> For when the priesthood is changed, **of necessity there takes place a change of law also.**—Hebrews 7:12 NASB

Therefore, upon Paul's conversion to Christianity, he switched his allegiance from the Torah to Jesus' Law—the Law of the Messianic King.

So what exactly is the Law of the Messianic King? What specific commandments are contained within it?

Chapter 7
Royal Law

The ancient city of Pergamum once thrived near modern day Turkey. The excavation of Pergamum shed unexpected light upon the precise scope of the Messianic King's Law.

Adolf Deissmann was the professor of Theology at the Ruprecht Karl University of Heidelberg at the height of Pergamum's excavation. He is best known for his pioneering work on the Koine Greek vocabulary used in the New Testament. In his work, *Light from the Ancient East*, Deissmann discusses what the archaeological discovery of his day revealed about the ancient Greek phrase, "the royal law":

> "The royal law," James 2:8, occurs also in the technical usage of the surrounding world. The law of astynomy at Pergamum, carved on stone in the time of Trajan but going back probably to a time before the Christian era, has a heading, formulated perhaps by the donor of the inscription in the time of Trajan, which says: τὸν βασιλικὸν νόμον ἐκ τῶν ἰδίων ἀνέθηκεν, "he set up the royal law out of his own means"

> I saw the original at Pergamum on Good Friday 1906. **The law is called "royal" because it was made by one of the kings of Pergamum."**

Deissmann explained that the Greek phrase "royal law" specifically referred to *laws issued by the king himself.* Thanks to the excavation of Pergamum, modern scholars now understand the significance of the phrase "royal law":

> To say that a law is "royal," however, is to say that it is a king's law.—Russell Pregeant (Emeritus Professor of Religion and Chaplain at Curry College

and Lecturer in New Testament at Andover Newton Theological School).[44]

The phrase "royal law" is found in one of the most critical sentences in the entire New Testament:

> If, however, you are fulfilling the royal law according to the Scripture, "YOU SHALL LOVE YOUR NEIGHBOR AS YOURSELF," you are doing well.[45]

It is rather unfortunate that modern Bibles leave the phrase unexplained in their translations. For James used the technical term "royal law" to deliver a specific and profound message to his first-century audience:

> If you are fulfilling the King's Law according to the scripture, "Love your neighbor as yourself," you are behaving properly.[46]

Readers of modern Bibles don't know that "royal laws" were laws made by the king himself. Therefore, they miss the significance of James' words. They do not realize that James was writing that the Law of the Messianic King is the scripture, "Love your neighbor as yourself."

> The adjective "royal" does not mean "fit for a king" but "of the king" and must mean that the law is understood by James as the law that governs the kingdom promised by Jesus to the poor. As far as James is concerned, it is the King's law that commands him to "love your neighbor as yourself."[47]— Patrick A. Tiller (Assistant Professor of New Testament at Harvard Divinity School)

The Law of the Messianic King (which replaced the Torah) contains only one precept, "Love your neighbor as yourself." This is why Paul wrote:

> The entire Law is fulfilled in one statement, in the precept, "Love your neighbor as yourself."[48]— Paul

---

44   *Knowing Truth, Doing Good: Engaging New Testament Ethics* by Russell Pregeant, p. 290, Fortress Press, 2008
45   James 2:8 NASB
46   James 2:8 as translated by Dr. William Berg
47   "The Rich and Poor in James: An Apocalyptic Epic" by Patrick A. Tiller as found in *Conflicted Boundaries in Wisdom and Apocalypticism* by Lawrence Mitchell Wills, Benjamin Givens Wright, p.172, Society of Biblical Lit, 2005
48   Galatians 5:14

* * *

> He who loves others has fulfilled the Law because "don't commit adultery," "don't murder," "don't steal," "don't covet," and if there is any other commandment it is summed up in these words: "Love your neighbor as yourself."[49]—Paul

When Paul wrote those words, he was referring to the Law of the Messianic King. After all, the Torah isn't even remotely fulfilled by loving our neighbors as ourselves. The Torah requires circumcision, observance of the Sabbath, not eating shellfish, etc. But the Law of the Messianic King *is* the scripture, "Love your neighbor as yourself." This is the Law that Paul commanded his followers to be enslaved to:

> For those who keep the Torah's Jobs are under a curse... You are enslaved to one another through love because the entire Law is fulfilled in one statement, in the precept, "Love your neighbor as yourself."... Bear one another's burdens and thereby fulfill the Law of the Messianic King.[50]—Paul

Paul spends a great deal of time telling his converts in Galatia to avoid being under the Torah. Then he concludes his letter by reminding them that they are instead enslaved to the Law of the Messianic King, the Law which is fulfilled by loving our neighbors as ourselves.

We find that there is a vast difference between the modern religious rewrite of Paul and the actual man of history. The actual Paul of history believed:

Christians are enslaved to the Law of the Messianic King which is the scripture, "Love your neighbor as yourself."

The arrival of the Messianic King and his Law is the event that launched Christianity in the first place. Paul and James both went forth to convert others to accept Jesus as the Messianic King and subject themselves to his Law: "Love your neighbor as yourself."

But where did Paul and James get this idea from in the first place? When did Jesus ever say that he had replaced the Torah with "Love your neighbor as yourself"?

---

49   Romans 13:8b-9
50   Galatians 3:10, 5:13b-14, 6:2

Chapter 8

Detour

The ancient religious leaders often referred to the Age of the Messianic King as "the age to come." They continually repeated one singular thought *ad nauseam*: Keeping the Torah is the way to have life in the age to come.

> He who acquires for himself the words of the Torah acquires for himself the life of the age to come.[51]

* * *

> Torah brings man into the life of the age to come.[52]

* * *

> To those who practice it, the Torah gives life in this age and in the age to come.[53]

Keeping the Torah is the way to life. Keeping the Torah is the way to life. Keeping the Torah is the way to life. That's what was drummed into the minds of the masses during Jesus' day:

> It was a commonplace in rabbinic teachings that the study of the Torah would lead to "life in the age to come."—George Eldon Ladd (Professor of New Testament Exegesis and Theology at Fuller Theological Seminary)[54]

---

51 P. Aboth 2.7
52 *Sifre Bemidbar* 37b-40a as found in *The Consequences of the Covenant*, p. 138, Brill Archive
53 P. Aboth 6.7
54 *A Theology of the New Testament* by George Eldon Ladd, p. 292, Wm. B. Eerdmans Publishing, 1993

* * *

The Torah was seen both as "the way of life and the way to life"—James D. G. Dunn (Lightfoot Professor of Divinity in the Department of Theology at the University of Durham)[55]

References to the Torah as the way to life abound in ancient rabbinic literature. Why am I also repeating this *ad nauseam*? Because I know of no better way to help you understand how provocative and shocking Jesus' teaching was from a first-century Jewish perspective.

> In everything, therefore, **treat people the same way you want them to treat you,** for this is the Law and the Prophets. **Enter through the narrow gate**; for the gate is wide and the way is broad that leads to destruction, and there are many who enter through it. For **the gate is small and the way is narrow that leads to life**, and there are few who find it.[56]

Can you imagine the dropping jaws? This teaching was specifically worded to fly in the face of the central teaching of the religious leaders. Jesus declared that the Golden Rule *is the way to life*. (Thus, the Torah is not.)

From a first-century Jewish perspective, Jesus' message was loud and clear. Those who follow the Golden Rule are on the road to life. Everyone else is on the road to destruction. Keeping the Torah isn't the deciding factor; the Golden Rule is.

The Golden Rule was a well-known principle in first-century Judea. For example, the Golden Rule is found in an ancient Aramaic commentary on the Biblical book of Leviticus.

> Leviticus 19:18—Love your neighbor as yourself: **Whatever you find hateful do not do to another.**[57]

The ancient Aramaic commentaries were called *targums*. The Leviticus Targum shows that the Golden Rule was the official way to fulfill Leviticus 19:18. During Jesus and Paul's day, the Golden Rule and Leviticus 19:18 were interchangeable:

55   *The New Perspective on Paul* by James D. G. Dunn, p. 74, Wm. B. Eerdmans Publishing, 2007
56   Matthew 7:12-14 NASB
57   Leviticus Targum, entry for Leviticus 19:18

Rabbi Akiva is presented in rabbinic sources as having voiced both the biblical love command (Lev. 19:18) and the Golden Rule as the fundamental and essential rule of the Law. Apparently, then, the Golden Rule came to be understood as an alternative form of the biblical "you shall love your neighbor as yourself" (Lev. 19:18).—Hubertus Waltherus Maria van de Sandt (Lecturer in New Testament Studies, Tilburg Faculty of Theology)[58]

Taking the Aramaic Targum and the rabbinic writings together, we come to one inescapable realization:

Judaism turned the golden rule into a somewhat different formulation of "Love your neighbor as yourself."—David Flusser (Professor of Early Christianity and Judaism of the Second Temple Period at the Hebrew University of Jerusalem)[59]

Knowing the ancient relationship between the Golden Rule and Leviticus 19:18 allows us to understand exactly why Paul and James taught what they did. It was Jesus' famous Sermon on the Mount that informed them that the Law of the Messianic King is Leviticus 19:18:

In everything, therefore, **treat people the same way you want them to treat you,** for this is the Law and the Prophets. **Enter through the narrow gate**; for the gate is wide and the way is broad that leads to destruction, and there are many who enter through it. For **the gate is small and the way is narrow that leads to life**, and there are few who find it.[60]

Jesus' followers were waiting for him to replace the Torah with the Law of the Messianic King. And Jesus fulfilled their expectation: he declared that keeping Leviticus 19:18 via the Golden Rule *is the way to life*... the Torah is not. In that moment, his followers understood that the Torah had finally been replaced with the Law of the Messianic King—"Love your neighbor as yourself."

In that moment, Jesus forced his listeners to take sides. Do they have faith in him and believe that loving your neighbor as yourself is the way to life? Or do they continue to try to find life by keeping the Torah? The first Christians were Jews who believed in Jesus, and therefore, taught others that they must be enslaved to the command to

---

58   *The Didache: Its Jewish Sources and Its Place in Early Judaism and Christianity* by Hubertus Waltherus Maria van de Sandt, Huub Van de Sandt, David Flüsser, p. 160, Fortress Press, 2002
59   *Judaism of the Second Temple Period: The Jewish Sages and Their Literature* by David Flusser, Azzan Yadin, p. 178, Wm. B. Eerdmans Publishing, 2009
60   Matthew 7:12-14 NASB

"Love your neighbor as yourself" if they want to have life.

But now, we come to yet another dilemma in understanding Paul. On the one hand, he says that the Torah was put in place only until the arrival of the Messianic King. On the other hand, he says that the Christian Faith doesn't abolish the Law:

> Does the Faith nullify the law? Certainly not! On the contrary, we preserve the law.[61]

So which one is it? Was the Torah put in place only until the arrival of the Messianic King? Or does the Christian Faith preserve the Law? How can both be true?

---

61   Romans 3:31

Chapter 9

Justices and Jobs

The apostle Paul belonged to the most popular Jewish sect of his day—the Pharisees. In fact, he was educated directly by Gamaliel, the head of the Pharisaic School of Hillel:

> I am a Jew, born in Tarsus of Cilicia, but brought up in this city, educated under Gamaliel, strictly according to the law of our fathers, being zealous for God just as you all are today.[62]—Paul

As a Pharisee, Paul thought of the Torah in terms of two separate groups of commandments: Justices and Jobs.[63] The Justices of the Torah included all the commandments between man and man. The Jobs of the Torah included all the commandments between man and God:

> Jewish tradition makes a distinction between *mitzvot bein adam la-Mokom*—commandments between a person and God—and *mitzvot bein adam la-chavero*—commandments between one person and another.—Central Conference of American Rabbis[64]

* * *

---

62   Acts 22:3 NASB
63   The English terms "Justices" and "Jobs" are in consonance with Paul's terms for the two great divisions of the Torah. "Justices" translates the Greek *dikaiomata*, while "Jobs" translates the Greek *erga*, literally "works." "Justices of the Torah" (*dikaiomata tou nomou*) is used by Paul in Romans 2:26; "Jobs of the Torah" (*erga tou nomou*) is used by Paul in Romans 3:20.
64   *Gates of Mitzvah: A Guide to the Jewish Life Cycle* by Simeon J. Maslin and Central Conference of American Rabbis, p. 97, CCAR Press, 1979

The traditional division of laws is *bein adam le-havero*, between man and his fellow man, and *bein adam la-makom*, between man and God.—Joseph Dov Soloveitchik (acclaimed Talmudic scholar)[65]

* * *

The Jewish law[66], however, like the Torah itself, is not limited to ethical conduct, *mitzvot bein adam lachaveiro*, "commandments between man and man." In fact, much of Jewish law deals with ritual and ceremony, *mitzvot bein adam lamakom*, "commandments between man and God."—Robert Gordis (President of the Rabbinical Assembly and the Synagogue Council of America and prior professor at Jewish Theological Seminary of America)[67]

Jesus, Paul, and their original audience all thought about the Law in terms of Justices and Jobs. The Justices included commands such as "Do not murder," "Do not steal," and "Do not commit adultery." The Jobs included commands such as "Be circumcised," "Observe the Sabbath," and "Don't eat shellfish."

In essence, there are two types of commandments found in the Torah: those concerning the relationship between man and God, and those concerning the relationship between man and man. The observance of the Sabbath[68] and the dietary regulations[69] are examples of commandments between man and God. The prohibitions against stealing, murder, slander, and causing embarrassment are examples of commandments between man and man.—Rabbi Prero[70]

There is a very easy way to determine whether a commandment is a Justice or a Job. All the Justices are based on "Love your neighbor as yourself."

Rabbi Pinchas states that **"all of the commandments between man and man are included in this precept of loving one's neighbor."**[71]—Rabbi Pinchas was one of the greatest Talmudists (Jewish legal scholars) of all time. His scholarly research is still studied and quoted to this day.

65   *The Emergence of Ethical Man* by Joseph Dov Soloveitchik, Michael S. Berger, p. 198, KTAV Publishing House, Inc
66   "*Halakhah*" in the text
67   *The Dynamics of Judaism: A Study in Jewish Law* by Robert Gordis, p. 63
68   "laws of *Shabbos*"
69   "laws of *kashrus*"
70   *Days of Celebration, Days of Inspiration* by Rabbi Yehudah Z. Prero, p. 41, Targum Press, 2006
71   *Judaism and Global Survival* by Richard H. Schwartz, p. 14, Lantern Books, 2002

If a commandment is based on "Love your neighbor as yourself," then it is a Justice. Otherwise, it is a Job.[72]

When Jesus taught that Leviticus 19:18 is the whole Law, he was saying that only the Justices are the Law. (The Jobs are not.) This is what separated the Christian sect from all the other Jewish sects. All

---

72   The Jewish nation divided their commandments into two groups: commandments between man and God (*mitzvot bein adam lamakom*) and commandments between man and man (*mitzvot bein adam lachaveiro*). (mishna Yoma 8:9) Philo documents that the commandments between man and God included all the piety and purity regulations; whereas the commandments between man and man included ethics and justice (Special Laws 2.63).

Philo further explained that the commands between man and God are encapsulated by love of God and the commands between man and man are encapsulated in love of neighbor (Decalogue 108-110). Philo presents this dual division of the law based on the two love commandments "as though obvious or well-known." (*Resurrecting Jesus: The Earliest Christian Tradition and Its Interpreters* by Dale C. Allison, p. 154, Continuum International Publishing Group, 2005).

The notion that the two love commands (love God and love neighbor) encompass all of God's commandments is presumed throughout the *Testament of the Twelve Patriarchs* (*t. Issachar* 5:2, 7:6-7; *t. Dan* 5:1-3; *t. Gad* 4:1-2; *t. Jos* 11:1; *t. Benj.* 3:-1-3; *t. Reub.* 6:8-9). Of particular note is *t. Dan* 5:1-3, "Observe, therefore, my children, the commandments of the Lord, and keep His law... Love the Lord through all your life, and one another with a true heart." The New Testament further documents that the ancient Jewish nation considered the two love commands (love God and love neighbor) to encompass all of God's commandments. Luke 10:26-27, "And Jesus asked the expert in the law, 'What is written in the law? How do you read it?' And the legal expert answered, 'You shall love the Lord your God with all your heart, and with all your soul, and with all your strength, and with all your mind; and your neighbor as yourself.'"

That the commands based on Leviticus 19:18 ("Love your neighbor as yourself") were an independent group of commands is further documented in multiple sources. For example, Hillel, the head of one of the greatest Pharisaic schools, stated that the Golden Rule (which was interchangeable with Leviticus 19:18 during his day) contained within it all the commands that a Gentile convert must follow (*t. Shabbos* 31a). Jesus referenced the commands based on Leviticus 19:18 as an independent group (Matthew 19:16-20). Paul referenced the commands based on Leviticus 19:18 as an independent group (Romans 13:9).

James declared Leviticus 19:18 to be the Messianic King's Law, and then proceeded to give examples of Old Testament commandments based upon it—commands such as "Do not murder," "Do not commit adultery," and "Don't show favoritism" (James 2:8-10). Murder and adultery were forbidden in the Decalogue and showing favoritism was forbidden in Leviticus 19:15. James' entire letter deals exclusively with Old Testament commands based on Leviticus 19:18 and is structured around this concept.

For documentation regarding James' assertion that Leviticus 19:18 is the Messianic King's Law, see chapter 7, "Royal Law".

As for the label "Jobs of the Torah," Paul and the Dead Sea Scrolls referred to the commandments that were done for God as "Jobs of the Torah" (Romans 3:20, Dead Sea Scroll 4QMMT).

As for the label "Justices of the Torah," Paul referred to the commandments that were done out of love of neighbor as "Justices of the Torah" (*dikaiomata tou nomou*). (Romans 2:26) For further documentation of the term "Justices of the Torah," see chapter 23, "Oxymoron."

This work shall use Paul's labels for the two groups of commandments: "Jobs of the Torah" and "Justices of the Torah."

the other Jewish sects considered both the Justices and the Jobs to be the Law. Christians, however, only considered the Justices to be the Law. For Christians, only the commandments based on "Love your neighbor as yourself" were the Law:

> He who loves others has fulfilled the Law because "don't commit adultery," "don't murder," "don't steal," "don't covet," and if there is any other commandment it is summed up in these words: "Love your neighbor as yourself."[73]—Paul

Notice that Paul specifies that only the commandments based on Leviticus 19:18 are the Law. In other words, only the Justices are the Law. This informs us of Paul's most central theology:

Because of the Law of the Messianic King ("Love your neighbor as yourself"), only the Justices are the Law.

Was the Torah superseded by the Law of the Messianic King? Yes, it was. However, did the Law of the Messianic King preserve the Torah's Justices? Yes, it preserved all of them. Therefore, the Christian Faith doesn't abolish the Law; rather, it preserves the Law:

> Does the Faith nullify the law? Certainly not! On the contrary, we preserve the law.[74]—Paul

"Do not murder" was preserved. "Do not steal" was preserved. "Do not commit adultery" was preserved. In fact, all the commandments based on Leviticus 19:18 were preserved.

The fact that the Law of the Messianic King preserved all the Torah's Justices can cause Paul's legal discussions to appear contradictory to the uninformed. Paul can talk about the Torah being replaced on the one hand, while immediately affirming the eternalness of the Torah on the other. The moment a person understands the preservation of the Torah's Justices, Paul's writings are very straightforward. This goes for Jesus' teachings too. Take Jesus' Sermon on the Mount as an example:

> I have not come to abolish the law, but to fulfill it…. In everything, therefore, treat people the same way you want them to treat you, for this is the law.[75]

---

73   Romans 13:8b-9
74   Romans 3:31
75   Matthew 5:17, 7:12

In first-century Jewish lingo, Jesus declared, "I haven't come to abolish the Law because only the Justices are the Law." He taught that keeping the Justices via the Golden Rule is the narrow road to life. This was the whole point of his famous Sermon on the Mount.

The relationship between the Justices and "life in the age to come" was the very core of Jesus' message:

> And someone came to him and said, "Teacher, which good thing must I do that I may have the life of the age to come?"
>
> But he answered him, "Why are you asking me about what is good? There is only one who is good. But **if you want to enter into that life, keep the commandments.**"
>
> **The man said to him, "Which ones?"**
>
> **And Jesus said, "Don't murder, don't commit adultery, don't steal, don't lie, honor your father and mother—love your neighbor as yourself."**[76]

Jesus singled out the commandments based on "Love your neighbor as yourself" as his sole requirement for "life in the age to come." He repeated the message from the Sermon on the Mount: Anyone who keeps the Justices is on the narrow road to life.

So if the Justices are God's entire law, then what did Paul conclude about the Jobs (such as circumcision)?

> Circumcision is nothing, and uncircumcision is nothing, but what matters is the keeping of the commandments of God.[77]—Paul

According to Paul, *the Jobs of the Torah aren't commandments of God.* And how could they be? After all, Jesus repeatedly taught that the Justices are the *entire* Law.

---

76   Matthew 19:16-19
77   1 Corinthians 7:19 NASB

Chapter 10

Jobless

Three of the more popular Justices were the commandments to "feed the hungry," "shelter the homeless," and "clothe the naked":

> Divide your bread with the hungry
> And bring the homeless poor into the house;
> When you see the naked, cover him[78]

These Justices are mentioned often in early Jewish writings. The ancient Jews recognized that the way to keep them is to practice *dikaiosune*:

> And for all those who **practice *dikaiosune*** from out of your possessions give your alms… **Give of your bread to the hungry one, and from your clothing to the naked ones**; make an almsgiving from everything that you have more than enough for you.[79]

Practicing *dikaiosune* and keeping the Justices were two sides of the same coin. To practice *dikaiosune* is to keep the Justices. To keep the Justices is to practice *dikaiosune*. It's no wonder why *dikaiosune* was one of Paul's favorite words!

Every Christian would do well to become familiar with the following two terms from the Greek word group to which *dikaiosune* belongs:

---

78   Isaiah 58:7 NASB
79   Tobit 4:6-7, 16

Dikaiosune	Justice
	Fairness
	Altruism
	Loving kindness
Dikaioi	Those who practice justice
	Those who practice fairness
	Those who practice altruism
	Those who practice loving kindness

Look how Jesus described the *dikaioi* in his quintessential teaching on judgment:

> But when the Son of Man comes in his majesty, and all the angels with him, then he will sit on his majestic throne. All the nations will be gathered before him and he will separate them from one another just as the shepherd separates the sheep from the goats. And he will place the sheep on his right and the goats on the left.

> Then the king will say to those on his right, "Come here! you who are blessed of my father, take possession of the kingdom held for you from the foundation of the world because **I was hungry and thirsty, and you gave me food and drink; I was a stranger and you invited me in; I was naked and you clothed me; I was sick and you visited me**; I was in prison and you came to me."

> **Then those who practiced altruism [*dikaioi*]** will reply to him, "Your highness, **when did we see you hungry and feed you, or thirsty and give you something to drink? And when did we see you a stranger and invite you in, or naked and clothe you?** When did we see you sick, or in prison, and come to visit you?"

> The king will answer saying to them, "I assure you that as much as you did it to one of these brothers of mine, the lowest in society, you did it to me."

Jesus taught the inextricable relationship between keeping the Justices and practicing *dikaiosune*. Those who feed the hungry, shelter the homeless, and clothe the naked are "those who practice altruism." In other words, those who keep the Justices are the ones who practice *dikaiosune*.

Sadly, conventional Bibles shove "righteousness" into Jesus' teaching on altruism:

> Then **the righteous** will answer Him, "Lord, when did we see You hungry, and feed You, or thirsty, and give You something to drink?"[80]

The translators refuse to acknowledge the altruism aspect of *dikaioi,* even when the topic is feeding the hungry, clothing the naked, and sheltering the homeless. They are so obsessed with "righteousness" that they obstinately betray the topic at hand. They wrongly characterize Jesus and Paul as hyper-focused on righteousness, instead of loving kindness and altruism.

In his quintessential teaching on judgment, Jesus taught that those who keep the Justices inherit the kingdom, while those who don't keep the Justices inherit the fire:

> And then he will say to those on his left, "**Go away from me, accursed ones, into the fire of the age** which has been held for the devil and his angels **because I was hungry and you gave me nothing to eat; I was thirsty and you gave me nothing; I was a stranger and you did not invite me in; naked, and you did not clothe me**; sick, and in prison, and you didn't visit me."[81]

Only the Justices matter. The Jobs count for nothing. In other words, Jesus taught that *no one will be vindicated before God by the Jobs of the Torah.*

Paul taught his converts the same thing:

> No one will be vindicated before God by the Jobs of the Torah.[82]—Paul

Modern Christians aren't told that the ancient Pharisees divided the Law into two groups of commandments demarcated by Leviticus 19:18. Therefore, they wrongly think that Paul wrote that no one will be vindicated by the Law. Yet that isn't what he wrote. He wrote that no one will be vindicated by the Jobs' group of the law. This is critical. While the Jobs are out, the Justices remain forever.

---

80   Matthew 25:37 NASB
81   Matthew 25:31-46
82   Romans 3:20

Chapter 11

Gezera Shava: the Missing Link

Paul understood that the Law of the Messianic King contained only the Justices and it *freed humanity from all the Jobs.*

- Is "Be circumcised" part of the Messianic King's Law? No.

- Is "Observe the Sabbath" part of the Messianic King's Law? No.

- Is "Don't eat shellfish" part of the Messianic King's Law? No.

- Is "Don't wear garments made of two cloths" part of the Messianic King's Law? No.

- Were festival observances part of the Messianic King's Law? No.

- And so on, and so on.

This concept was almost impossible for first-century Jews to accept. A Dead Sea Scroll, found in cave four, revealed that many ancient Jews believed that keeping the Jobs of the Torah was absolutely necessary for vindication before God:

> **We have sent you some of the Jobs of the Torah** which we have discerned will be for your good and for the good of your people. For we recognize that you have wisdom and knowledge of the law. Consider all these things and

ask God to strengthen your will and keep you away from evil thoughts and from Belial's counsel. Then you will rejoice at the end of time when you will find some of our judgments to be correct. **And it will be credited to you as vindication.**[83]

The ancient Jews were raised to believe that keeping the Jobs of the Torah was the basis of their vindication before God. But believing in Jesus meant that they had to trust that only the Justices are the Law. If Jesus was wrong, then they would lose their souls for believing in him. If he was right, they would lose their souls if they continued trying to be vindicated by the Jobs of the Torah. What a dilemma!

The strong belief in vindication via the Jobs of the Torah was one of the biggest issues that Paul faced in his ministry. In fact, his entire letter to the Galatians was written to address this one singular issue. Paul had taught his converts to enslave themselves to the Law of the Messianic King—"Love your neighbor as yourselves." However, some well-meaning Jews started convincing the Galatians that the Jobs of the Torah were essential for salvation, as well. Therefore, many began enslaving themselves to Jobs, such as festival observances.

> Now, however, that you know God, or rather are known by God, how is it that you turn once again to weak and impoverished entities whom you're willing to serve as slaves all over again? **You're still observing their holidays and months and seasons and years! I'm afraid I've somehow wasted my effort on you.**[84]

The Galatians' enslavement to the Jobs was a direct rejection of the Messianic King's Law, the Law intended to free humanity from the Jobs. Therefore, if the Galatians remained enslaved to the Jobs of the Torah, then Paul had wasted his effort on them. So he wrote a letter to warn the Galatians that anyone who lives his life based on the Jobs of the Torah is under a curse:

> For all who are operating out of the Jobs of the Torah are under a curse.[85]

But Paul knew that he had to do more than just state this warning. After all, the well-meaning Jews thought that they were

---

83   Dead Sea Scroll 4QMMT
84   Galatians 4:9-11
85   Galatians 3:10

teaching the Gentiles what the scriptures really say. Paul needed to find a way to *prove from scripture* that Jesus had freed humanity from the Jobs of the Torah. He needed to prove this in a way that his Jewish opposition would understand and believe. Therefore, to successfully counter the opposition, Paul chose to use a popular first-century Jewish technique called *Gezera Shava*:

> *Gezera Shava* holds when two passages contain words that are similar or have identical connotations, the laws of the two passages are subject to the same regulations and applications.—George Robinson (Dr. Robinson is a contributor to the forthcoming revised edition of the *Encyclopaedia Judaica*. He has received the Simon Rockower Award for excellence in Jewish journalism from the American Jewish Press Association.) [86]

Gezera Shava is actually very easy to understand. The phrase simply means "equivalent pronouncements." According to this principle, any two scriptures that share a word or phrase in common can be treated as "equal pronouncements." Oddly, the two scriptures don't have to have anything else in common except for the sharing of a word or phrase. For example, consider the following two scriptures:

> Esau came in from the **field**[87]

> * * *

> if in the **field** the man finds the girl who is engaged, and the man forces her and lies with her, then only the man who lies with her shall die.[88]

According to *Gezera Shava*, Esau is the same as the man who rapes the betrothed maiden because both scriptures share the same word "field." Does this defy all logic? Yes. But is this the way that the ancient Jewish people interpreted these scriptures? Yes.

> "Esau came in from the field." That means, he had sexual relations with a betrothed girl, in line with this verse: "But if the man find the damsel that is betrothed in the field and the man take hold of her and lie with her" (Deut 22:25)—Genesis Rabbah (an ancient Jewish explanation of the Biblical book of Genesis)[89]

86   *Essential Judaism: A Complete Guide to Beliefs, Customs and Rituals* by George Robinson, p. 316, Simon and Schuster, 2001
87   Genesis 25:29b NASB
88   Deuteronomy 22:25 NASB
89   *Genesis Rabbah* 63.12 as quoted in *Jeremiah in Talmud and Midrash: A Source Book* by Jacob Neusner, p. 117, University Press of America, 2006

An ancient Jewish explanation of Genesis states that Esau raped a betrothed maiden because of the *Gezera Shava* on the word "field." According to *Gezera Shava*:

> Esau who came in from the field
> > *Is the same as* the man who rapes a betrothed maiden in the field.

Esau's act of rape, discovered by *Gezera Shava*, was accepted by the Jews as scriptural fact:

> wicked Esau was to commit two grievous transgressions: he was to rape a maiden who was betrothed and he was to murder to human being. Of the first of these transgressions it is written *And Esau came in from the field* (Gen. 25:29). **That Esau was guilty of rape is shown by the fact that the verse specifying his coming in *from the field* is linked with another verse also specifying "field," the verse from Deuteronomy that states the penalty for rape: "If the man find the damsel that is betrothed in the field"** (Deut. 22:25).[90]—William Gordon Braude (Rabbi Braude taught at Brown, Yale, and Hebrew University in Jerusalem.)

Thanks to *Gezera Shava*, Esau's act of rape was part and parcel of Jewish belief:

> **Esau violated a betrothed maiden** and committed murder—Sander L. Gilman (previous professor at Cornell University who later founded the Program in Jewish Studies at the University of Illinois)[91]

* * *

> Esau committed three abominations–**violating a betrothed maiden**, murder, and theft—Louis H. Feldman (Professor of Classics at Yeshiva University)[92]

* * *

> For some time Esau had been pursuing his evil inclinations in secret. Finally he dropped his mask, and on the day of Abraham's death he was guilty of five crimes: **he ravished a betrothed maiden**, committed murder, doubted the resurrection of the dead, scorned the birthright, and denied God.—Louis Ginzberg (a Talmudist[93] and leading figure in the Conservative Movement

90   *Pĕsiḳta dĕ-Rab̲ Kahăna: R. Kahana's Compilation of Discourses for Sabbaths and Festal Days* by William Gordon Braude, Israel James Kapstein Jewish Publication Society, 2002
91   *Anti-Semitism in Times of Crisis* by Sander L. Gilman, Steven T. Katz, p. 111, NYU Press, 1993
92   *Josephus's Interpretation of the Bible* by Louis H. Feldman, p. 316, University of California Press, 1998
93   Talmudist: a scholar of ancient Jewish law

of Judaism of the twentieth century)[94]

This example illustrates that any two scriptures, even those that have no topic in common, could be joined together as equivalents via *Gezera Shava*.[95] This was the Jewish culture in which Paul was raised, and this was the Jewish culture to which he wrote.

With this in mind, let's reexamine Paul's dilemma with the Galatians. Some Jews told the Galatians that they must obey the entire Torah, not only the Justices. How could Paul convince them that they were wrong? He could do this by applying *Gezera Shava* to the following two scriptures:

> **Accursed** is everyone who is hung on wood.

> * * *

> **Accursed** is everyone who does not abide by all that has been written in the book of the Torah.

Both scriptures have the same word: 'accursed.' Therefore, they can be considered "equal pronouncements" via *Gezera Shava*. In other words, 'the accursed person being hung on wood' could be considered to be the embodiment of the curse of having to keep everything written in the Torah. In this way, Paul could use these scriptures to show that Jesus being hung on wood was the embodiment of the curse of having to keep everything written in the Torah. Therefore, Jesus became the curse of having to keep the entire Torah on our behalf.

> For all who are operating from the Jobs of the Torah are under a curse. For it is written: "**Accursed is everyone who does not abide by all that has**

---

94   *The Legends of the Jews: From the Creation to Jacob* by Louis Ginzberg, p. 318, Cosimo, Inc., 2006

95   The *Genesis Rabbah* explanation of Esau documents that *Gezera Shava* wasn't restricted to legal texts. Furthermore, Dead Sea Scrolls 4Q174 and 4Q177 contain numerous instances where various Psalms are interpreted relative to the Prophets via a shared catchword. Neither Psalms nor the Prophets were legal texts. These scrolls document that *Gezera Shava* was routinely applied to non-legal texts during Paul's and Jesus' day. (See *Ethics in the Qumran Community* by Marcus K. M. Tso, p. 96, Mohr Siebeck, 2010.) Also, Dead Sea Scroll 1QS V, 17 used Isaiah 2:22 within a *Gezera Shava*. Scholars have marveled that this scroll applied *Gezera Shava* to both legal and "non-legal" scriptures, which is fully consistent with the New Testament authors.

The earliest known instance of *Gezera Shava* has been found in Ben Sirach's writings (2nd century BCE). (See *The Origin of the Samaritans* by Magnar Kartveit, p. 144, BRILL, 2009.) This example even predates Hillel, the eminent Pharisee who conceived the term *Gezera Shava*. Hillel taught the generation that preceded Jesus and Paul.

been written in the book of the Torah…." The Messianic King redeemed us from the curse of the Torah, having become the curse on our behalf—for it is written, "<u>Accursed</u> is everyone who is hung on wood"[96]—Paul

This is precisely the approach Paul took. He applied *Gezera Shava* to those very scriptures in order to *prove from scripture* that:

> Jesus (who became a curse by hanging on wood)
> > *Is the same as* the curse of having to keep the entire Torah.
> > > *Therefore,* Jesus freed humanity from having to keep the entire Torah by becoming that curse on our behalf.

Dr. Frederick Fyvie Bruce describes it this way:

> As Paul quotes Dt. 21:23 ["Accursed is anyone hung on wood"], it shares a common term with Dt. 27:26 ["Accursed is everyone who does not abide by all that has been written in the book of the Torah"], and thus provides an instance of the exegetical principle known to the rabbis as *gezerah shawah* ("equal category")…. Paul's present use of *gezerah shawah* is based on the Greek version—Frederick Fyvie Bruce (Dr. Bruce was one of the founders of the modern evangelical understanding of the Bible. After teaching Greek for several years, first at the University of Edinburgh, and then at the University of Leeds, he became head of the Department of Biblical History and Literature at the University of Sheffield. He also served as professor of Biblical Criticism and Exegesis. At different times, Bruce was elected as president of the (British) Society for New Testament Studies and the Society for Old Testament Studies. He is one of a handful of scholars thus recognized by his peers in both fields.)[97]

It was through the popular Jewish principle of *Gezera Shava* that Paul proved that humanity no longer has to keep the entire Torah, only the Justices.

Gezera Shava is used throughout the New Testament. Paul used it. Matthew used it. The author of Hebrews used it. Jesus used it. As you have just seen, even the most crucial theologies of the New Testament are all based on *Gezera Shava*. I promise that once you become familiar with it, you will never look at the New Testament in the same way again.

It should be noted that *Gezera Shava* is an English transliteration

---

96   Galatians 3:10, 13 as translated by Dr. William Berg
97   *The Epistle to the Galatians: A Commentary on the Greek Text* by Frederick Fyvie Bruce, p. 165, Wm. B. Eerdmans Publishing, 1982 (bracketed quotations added by author — M.W.)

of a Hebrew phrase. Therefore, there are a number of different ways to spell it.

It can be spelled *Gezerah Shawah*:

Gezerah Shawah: "Equal law/statute" or an argument from analogy. Biblical passages containing synonyms or homonyms are subject, however much they differ in other respects, to identical definitions and applications.—Leo G. Perdue (Professor of Hebrew Bible at Brite Divinity School)[98]

It can be spelled *Gezerah Shavah*:

The writer can introduce Psalms 8:4-6 naturally on the basis of the Jewish interpretive rule, *gezerah shavah*, the principle by which one was permitted to link key words or phrases.—Craig S. Keener (Professor of New Testament at Palmer Theological Seminary of Eastern University)[99]

It can be spelled *Gezera Shava*:

We learn by *gezera shava*, a decree of equivalence, that Leviticus 22:32, 'shall be sanctified in the midst of Israel,' is to be read in light of Numbers 16:21—The Rabbinical Assembly of America[100]

And there are numerous other ways to spell it as well.

I've included these references not only to illustrate the various spellings, but also to demonstrate how extremely familiar Biblical scholars are with *Gezera Shava*. In fact, the Rabbinical Council of America nonchalantly acknowledges:

Every student of Talmud is familiar with this concept of *Gezera Shava* as utilized in a legal framework.[101]

The Talmud is the official collection of Jewish law and tradition. *Every* student of Talmud must be familiar with *Gezera Shava* because it's literally impossible to understand ancient Jewish discussions of scripture without it. Sadly, what is known by every student of Jewish history (and virtually every Biblical scholar) is virtually unknown to

98 *The Sword and the Stylus: An Introduction to Wisdom in the Age of Empires* by Leo G. Perdue p. 409, Wm. B. Eerdmans Publishing, 2008
99 *The IVP Bible Background Commentary: New Testament* by Craig S. Keener p. 653, InterVarsity Press, 1993
100   *Conservative Judaism, Volume 58* by Rabbinical Assembly of America, Rabbinical Assembly and the Jewish Theological Seminary of America, Rabbinical Assembly, 2005
101   *Tradition: Volume 24*, Rabbinical Council of America, 1988

most Christians sitting in the pew. Yet the New Testament is infused with *Gezera Shava* from beginning to end. Without an understanding of this concept, the most crucial theologies of the text are completely lost on the modern reader.

For example, Paul used *Gezera Shava* to prove that previously committed sins can be covered over via faith:[102]

> If Abraham was vindicated because of jobs, he has reason to boast — though not with God. But what does scripture say? **"Abraham trusted God, and it was <u>credited</u> to his account as vindication."**
>
> But wages are not credited to a worker's account as a favor but as something owed. As for one who isn't a worker but a believer in him who pronounces judgment on the impious, his faith is credited to his account as vindication.
>
> Likewise, David also tells of the happiness of the person to whose account God credits vindication with no jobs: **"Blessed is he whose violations of the law are forgiven, whose sin is covered; blessed is the man to whom the Lord does not <u>credit</u> sin."** —Paul[103]

Paul applied *Gezara Shava* to the following scriptures:

> Abraham believed God and it was **credited** to him as vindication.[104]

* * *

> Blessed are those whose legal violations and sins were covered over. Blessed is the man to whom in no way the Lord should **credit** sin.[105]

He used *Gezera Shava* to *prove from scripture*:

> The vindication credited to Abraham by faith
> > *Is the same as* the legal violations and sins not being credited.

Thus he used *Gezera Shava* to establish a most fundamental Christian belief: the forgiveness of previously committed sins by faith.[106]

---

102   Paul prefaced his discussion on Abraham with the declaration that Jesus' atonement covered previously committed sins. "Because in the forbearance of God He passed over the sins *previously* committed" (Romans 3:25 NASB).

103   Romans 4:2-8

104   Galatians 3:6

105   Psalm 32:1-2 LXX

106   Paul prefaced his discussion on Abraham with the declaration that Jesus' atonement covered

Paul connects a Davidic psalm (Ps 32:1-2) to Abraham's faith-reckoned righteousness by applying a rabbinic hermeneutical principle (*Gezera Shawa*) that allows for texts to be linked and interpreted based on a common word—David Capes (Professor in Christianity, Houston Baptist University)[107]

*   *   *

That the reference to David is complementary to the reference to Abraham is made evident by the "just as" with which verse 6 begins. Paul makes uses of the interpretive technique of *gezerah shewah* according to which two passages are linked together to make a single point when similar words are present.—Gerhard H. Visscher (Professor of New Testament, Canadian Reformed Theological Seminary)[108]

*   *   *

The gratuity of justification is underlined by the *gezerah shewa* introduced in 4:3-8: just as the forgiveness by which, according to Psalm 32:1-2, David's sin was not "counted" against him was an act of divine grace, so must be the justification by which Abraham was "counted" righteous in Genesis 15:6.[109]—Stephen Westerholm (Associate Professor, Department of Religious Studies, McMaster University)

Gezera Shava seems bizarre to modern readers because the principle defies the logical norms of all ancient and modern cultures. It was entirely unique to the ancient Jewish people. Many ancient Gentile Christians were unaware of it. Therefore they remained oblivious to many teachings of the New Testament, including Jesus' most profound, fundamental teaching. For Jesus' most profound, fundamental teaching was based on *Gezera Shava*, and it is unveiled in the following chapter.

---

previously committed sins. "Because in the forbearance of God He passed over the sins *previously committed*" (Romans 3:25 NASB).

107   *Rediscovering Paul: An Introduction to His World, Letters and Theology* by David B. Capes, Rodney Reeves, E. Randolph Richards, p. 183, InterVarsity Press, 2007

108   *Romans 4 and the New Perspective on Paul: Faith Embraces the Promise* by Gerhard H. Visscher, p. 182, Peter Lang, 2009

109   *Perspectives Old and New on Paul: The "Lutheran" Paul and His Critics* by Stephen Westerholm, p. 234, Wm. B. Eerdmans Publishing, 2004

Chapter 12

The Tables Have Turned

In all of Moses' writings, there were two scriptures that were particularly ideal for *Gezera Shava*:

> **You shall love** the Lord your God with all your heart, and with all your soul, and with all your mind.—Deuteronomy 6:5

* * *

> **You shall love** your neighbor as yourself.—Leviticus 19:18

The Hebrew form of "you shall love" is used almost nowhere else in the entire Old Testament. This made it a prime candidate for *Gezera Shava*:

> The same grammatical form of the term "love" is used in Deut 6:5 and Lev 19:18, however, **it appears almost nowhere else in the Old Testament. This opens for the use of** *Gezerah Shawa*[110]—Erik Waaler (Associate Professor with PhD in Religion; research focus: intertextuality of Matthew and archaeology of Ketef Hinnom)

How often is the Hebrew form of "you shall love" used in the Old Testament? This Hebrew form is only used for:

- You shall love God (Deut. 6:5, 11:1)

- You shall love others as yourself (Lev. 19:18, 34)

---

110   *The Shema and the First Commandment in First Corinthians: An Intertextual Approach to Paul's Re-reading of Deuteronomy*, by Erik Waaler PhD, Mohr Siebeck, 2008, p.222

In all of the Old Testament, this particular verbal form of "love" was only used for "You shall love God" and "You shall love others as yourself." That's it. This would have been impossible for the *Gezera Shava*-loving Jews to miss.

With this in mind, you are now ready to understand the most crucial showdown between the Pharisees and Jesus. The showdown is recorded in the Gospel of Matthew. Let's take a look at some of Jesus' teachings that led up to this point:

- *Chapter Seven*: Jesus taught that fulfilling Leviticus 19:18 via the Golden Rule is the way to life. (The Torah is not.)

- *Chapter Nineteen*: Jesus informs a wealthy young man that anyone who follows the commandments based on Leviticus 19:18 will inherit life.

Then, in chapter twenty-two, Jesus meets some Pharisees who are really upset about his Leviticus 19:18 teachings. They cannot believe that Jesus singled out "Love your neighbor as yourself" as if it is the only thing that matters. So they decided to set a trap for him.

In the first-century Jewish nation, "Love God with your whole being" was considered to be the greatest commandment. Anyone who refused to acknowledge this was branded a heretic. Therefore, the Pharisees believed that it would be easy to get Jesus to recant his teachings on "Love your neighbor as yourself."

> One of the Pharisees, **an expert in the Law**, asked Jesus a question to trap him. **"Teacher, what is the great commandment in the Law?"**[111]

The Pharisees believed that they had boxed Jesus into a corner. If Jesus affirmed that "Love God" is the greatest commandment, then he'd be admitting that "Love your neighbor" isn't the entire Law. However, if he said that "Love your neighbor as yourself" is the greatest commandment, then the Pharisees would have reason to stone him to death. Either way, they'd finally put Jesus out of commission once and for all.

---

111   Matthew 22:35-36

The Pharisees believed that their trap was bulletproof. However, Jesus used *Gezera Shava* to turn the tables and win the day:

> One of the Pharisees, an expert in the Law, asked Jesus a question to trap him. "Teacher, what is the great commandment in the Law?"
>
> **And Jesus said to him, "'<u>You shall love</u> the Lord your God with all your heart, and with all your soul, and with all your mind.' This is the great and first commandment. And the second is the same as it. '<u>You shall love</u> your neighbor as yourself.'"[112]**

Just as Paul used *Gezera Shava* to show:

> The curse of Jesus hanging on a tree
> > **Is the same as** the curse of having to keep the entire Torah

Just as Paul used *Gezera Shava* to show:

> The vindication credited to Abraham
> > **Is the same as** the legal violations and sins no longer credited

So too Jesus used *Gezera Shava* to show:

> The command to "Love your neighbor as yourself"
> > **Is the same as** the command to "Love God with your whole heart, soul, and mind."

Jesus used *Gezera Shava* to turn the tables and prove his point. He began by acknowledging that "You shall love God" is the foremost commandment. Then he used *Gezera Shava* to prove that "You shall love your neighbor" is identical to it.[113] In other words, loving your

---

112   Matthew 22:35-39

113   Matthew 22:39 uses the Greek word *homoia* combined with *Gezera Shava* to show that the second commandment is identical to the first. Dr. Berg's note: The adjective *homoios* (feminine *homoia*, neuter *homoion*) derives from *homos*, which means "one and the same" (see H. Frisk, *Griechisches etymologisches Wörterbuch* and P. Chantraine, *Dictionnaire etymologique de la langue grecque*, under the ὁμός-entries); *homoios*, likewise, signifies identity at one end of its spectrum of meaning, and similarity at the other end. For the most part, especially in first-century contexts, it leans toward the "upper" end of the spectrum, indicating equivalence, equality, congruence or the "perfect match." Its real force is best seen in Greek mathematics, from Euclid through Archimedes and Ptolemy and beyond, where congruent angles, triangles, polygons, etc. are called *isa kai homoia* ("equal and the same," "one and the same"). In that very common expression, *homoia* reinforces and emphasizes the equality specified in *isa* (the conventional translation, "equal and similar," fails to take note of that intensifying function). (For references, see Liddell-Scott-Jones, *Greek Lexicon*, under the entry ὅμοιος.) The fact that Matthew 22:37-40 uses *homoia* in the context of a *Gezera Shava* ("equivalent pronouncement") would indicate a semantic position in

neighbor as yourself is the total fulfillment of the command to "Love God with your whole heart, soul, and mind." Therefore, Leviticus 19:18—"Love your neighbor as yourself"—truly is the entire Law. Jesus won.

But Houston, we have a problem. Conventional Bibles make it appear that the Pharisees won and Jesus lost! According to modern translations, Jesus said that the second commandment "is like" the first:

> And Jesus said to him, "'YOU SHALL LOVE THE LORD YOUR GOD WITH ALL YOUR HEART, AND WITH ALL YOUR SOUL, AND WITH ALL YOUR MIND.' This is the great and foremost commandment.
>
> "**The second is like it**, 'YOU SHALL LOVE YOUR NEIGHBOR AS YOURSELF.'" [114]

Modern Bibles conceal that "Love your neighbor" is one and the same as "Love God." They hide the fact that Jesus considered the two commandments to be two ways of saying the very same thing. The books passed out in churches are BINOs—"Bibles In Name Only." They may call themselves Bibles, but their highly inventive rewrites betray the historical Jesus and Paul.

In Matthew, the sequence of events for the historical Jesus is:

- Jesus announces that Leviticus 19:18 has replaced the Torah as the way to life.[115]

- Then, Jesus informs a wealthy young man that anyone who keeps the commandments based on Leviticus 19:18 inherits life.[116]

- Then, Jesus teaches (via *Gezera Shava*) that Leviticus 19:18 is the total fulfillment of the command to "Love God with your whole heart, soul, and mind."[117]

- Then, Jesus teaches that every altruistic person who keeps the Justices—

---

the upper reaches of *homoios'* range of meaning, in the area of "equal" or "equivalent," or "the same." Therefore, the Greek text would support the premise that "Love your neighbor as yourself" is one and the same with "Love God with your whole being."

114   Matthew 22:37–39 NASB
115   Matthew 7:12-14
116   Matthew 19:16-19
117   Matthew 22:35-39

all the commandments based on Leviticus 19:18—will inherit the kingdom on judgment day.[118]

That's the consistent, repetitive teaching of Jesus of Nazareth in the original Gospel of Matthew. Yet here's the irony. Modern Bibles have correctly translated (more or less) the first, second, and fourth teachings in the sequence. However, they have completely mistranslated the third teaching. They claim that "Love God" is separate and greater than "Love your neighbor." How do modern Christian theologians deal with the contradiction introduced by this mistranslation? They embrace the mistranslation as the 'Word of God', and then use it to reject the three correctly translated teachings. Oops!

Jesus in Perspective

Chapter Seven:

> In everything, therefore, **treat people the same way you want them to treat you, for this is the Law** and the Prophets. **Enter through the narrow gate**; for the gate is wide and the way is broad that leads to destruction, and there are many who enter through it. **For the gate is small and the way is narrow that leads to life, and there are few who find it.**[119]

Chapter Nineteen

> And someone came to him and said, "Teacher, **which good thing must I do that I may have the life of the age to come?"**
>
> But he answered him, "Why are you asking me about what is good? There is only one who is good. But **if you want to enter into that life, keep the commandments."**
>
> **The man said to him, "Which ones?"**
>
> And Jesus said, **"Don't murder, don't commit adultery, don't steal, don't lie, honor your father and mother—love your neighbor as yourself."**[120]

Chapter Twenty-Two

> One of the Pharisees, an expert in the Law, asked Jesus a question to trap him. "Teacher, what is the great commandment in the Law?"

---

118   Matthew 25:31-46
119   Matthew 7:12-14 NASB
120   Matthew 19:16-19

And Jesus said to him, "'**You shall love the Lord your God with all your heart, and with all your soul, and with all your mind.' This is the great and first commandment. And the second is the same as it. 'You shall love your neighbor as yourself.'**"

Chapter Twenty-Five

When the Son of Man comes in his majesty, and all the angels with him, then he will sit on his majestic throne. All the nations will be gathered before him and he will separate them from one another just as the shepherd separates the sheep from the goats. And he will place the sheep on his right and the goats on the left.

Then the king will say to those on his right, "Come here! you who are blessed of my father, **take possession of the kingdom held for you from the foundation of the world, because I was hungry and thirsty, and you gave me food and drink; I was a stranger and you invited me in; I was naked and you clothed me; I was sick and you visited me; I was in prison and you came to me.**"

Then **those who practiced altruism** will reply to him, "Your highness, when did we see you hungry and feed you, or thirsty and give you something to drink? And when did we see you a stranger and invite you in, or naked and clothe you? When did we see you sick, or in prison, and come to visit you?"

The king will answer saying to them, "I assure you that as much as you did it to one of these brothers of mine, the lowest in society, you did it to me."

And then he will say to those on his left, "**Go away from me, accursed ones, into the fire of the age which has been held for the devil and his angels, because I was hungry and you gave me nothing to eat; I was thirsty and you gave me nothing; I was a stranger and you did not invite me in; naked, and you did not clothe me; sick, and in prison, and you didn't visit me.**"[121]

There is no contradiction in Matthew. The Gospel of Matthew repeatedly affirms one singular teaching: Only the Justices are the Law; the Jobs are not. It's no wonder that the earliest Christians chose the Gospel of Matthew as the first book of the New Testament. It is our introduction to the rest of the books, including the writings of Paul.

---

121   Matthew 25:31-46

Chapter 13

Mystical Union

Jesus' showdown with the Pharisees wasn't the only time when he taught that loving our neighbor is the same as loving God. He taught the same thing in his quintessential teaching on judgment as well:

> Then those who treated people altruistically will reply to him, "Your highness, when did we see you hungry and feed you, or thirsty and give you something to drink? And when did we see you a stranger and invite you in, or naked and clothe you? When did we see you sick, or in prison, and come to visit you?"
>
> The king will answer saying to them, "**I assure you that as much as you did it to one of these brothers of mine, the lowest in society, you did it to me.**"[122]

Anyone who serves his neighbor serves God in the process. And people who don't serve their neighbors are not serving God:

> Then they also will answer, "Your highness, when did we see you hungry, or thirsty, or a stranger, or naked, or sick, or in prison and did not be of service to you?'
>
> Then he will answer them saying, "**I assure you, as much as you didn't do it to the lowest of society, you didn't do it to me.**"[123]

To love others is to love God. This is the mystical union that Jesus taught via *Gezera Shava* in his showdown with the Pharisees.

122   Matthew 25:37-40
123   Matthew 25:44-45

He taught this in his quintessential teaching on judgment as well. So it's not surprising that the spiritual relationship between loving our neighbor and loving God was also taught by Paul:

> Thank God you were once slaves of sin, but now have obeyed from your hearts the type of teaching that you were brought over to! Having been emancipated from sin, **you've been enslaved to the just, fair, altruistic treatment of others**.... But now, freed from sin and **enslaved to God**, you have complete consecration as your harvest, and your result is life in the age to come.[124]

In Paul's theology, "enslavement to the just, fair, altruistic treatment of others" is the same as being "enslaved to God." He thoroughly embraced the spiritual relationship between loving our neighbor and loving God, which was taught by Jesus.

However, most of the references to this mystical union have been expunged from modern Bibles.

- Modern Bibles remove Jesus' use of *Gezera Shava* during his showdown with the Pharisees.

- Modern Bibles portray Paul as equating "enslavement to righteousness" with "enslavement to God."

- The most popular modern Bible, the NIV, has even removed the mystical union from Jesus' quintessential teaching on judgment as well![125]

There is an inseparable connection between the mystical union and the Law of the Messianic King. In his showdown with the Pharisees, Jesus taught that "Love your neighbor as yourself" is the entire Law *because of the mystical union*. That's the only way that Leviticus 19:18 could be the entire Law. Therefore, by removing the mystical union from modern Bibles, translators made it impossible for readers to know that Jesus had replaced the Torah with Leviticus 19:18—"Love your neighbor as yourself."

---

124   Romans 6:17-22
125   In Matthew 25:40 and 25:45, the NIV has Jesus saying that, whenever we are serving our neighbor, we are doing it for Jesus, not to him, like every other translation attests. In doing this, the NIV has removed the mystical union from Jesus' quintessential teaching on judgment.

Also, in some passages, it's impossible to see the mystical union without knowing *Gezera Shava*. Take Paul's list of those who misuse their body parts as an example:

> No one's seeking after God. Everyone together avoids him, becoming useless. There isn't anyone showing loving kindness, not even one. Their throat is an open tomb. They deceive with their tongues. The poison of snakes is under their lips; whose mouth is filled with curses and bitterness. Their feet are eager to shed blood. Destruction and misery lay in their paths. The way of peace they have never known. There is no reverence of God before their eyes.—Paul[126]

There is so much more going on in this passage than first meets the eye. Paul constructed this list from *six different Old Testament passages*:

1. No one's seeking after God. Everyone together avoids him, becoming useless. There isn't anyone showing loving kindness, not even one.[127]

2. Their throat is an open tomb. They deceive with their tongues.[128]

3. The poison of snakes is under their lips;[129]

4. Whose mouth is filled with curses and bitterness.[130]

5. Their feet are eager to shed blood. Destruction and misery lay in their paths. The way of peace they have never known.[131]

6. There is no reverence of God before their eyes.[132]

Paul didn't assemble the list arbitrarily. Quite the opposite, he created the list using *Gezera Shava*. For example, passages one and two are linked together via the key phrase, "there is no":

> From heaven, the Lord looked upon the sons of men, to see **if there was anyone who is** perceiving or **seeking after God. All have turned aside together, becoming useless.** <u>There is no</u> person acting kindly, not even one.

---

126   Romans 3:11-18
127   Psalms 14:1-3
128   Psalm 5:9
129   Psalm 140:3
130   Psalm 10:7
131   Isaiah 59:7,8
132   Psalm 36:1

* * *

For <u>there is no</u> truth in their mouth; their heart is futile; **their throat is an open tomb; they deceive with their tongues.**[133]

The bolded words are the ones that Paul used in his list. The underlined words are the key that Paul used to link the two passages together via *Gezera Shava*. Paul used *Gezera Shava* to show:

> Those who use their throats and tongues against others
>> ***Are the same ones*** who have turned away from God, becoming useless.

Paul equated "turning away from God" with "using your body parts for the mistreatment of others."

He continued using *Gezera Shava* to expand his list. Passages two and three are linked together via the keyword "tongue":

For there is no truth in their mouth; their heart is futile; **their throat is an open tomb; they deceive with their <u>tongues</u>.**[134]

* * *

They sharpened their <u>tongue</u> like a snake. **The poison of snakes is under their lips.**

Once again, the bolded words are the ones that Paul used in his list. The underlined words are the key that he used to link the passages together via *Gezera Shava*.

- "Those with the poison of snakes under their lips" are the same as "those whose throat is an open tomb, who deceive with their mouths" (via the keyword 'tongue').

- "Those whose throat is an open tomb, who deceive with their mouths" are the same as "those who are not seeking after God" (via the keywords "there is no").

Passages one and two share: "there is no."

Passages two and three share: "tongue."

---

133   Psalm 5:9 LXX
134   Psalm 5:9 LXX

Here are the keyword links for all six passages:

- Passages 1 and 2 are equal via the keywords "there is no."

- Passages 2 and 3 are equal via the keyword "tongue."

- Passages 3 and 4 are equal via the keyword "tongue."

- Passages 4 and 5 are equal via the keyword "innocent."

- Passages 5 and 6 are equal via the keyword "iniquity."

Do you see how steeped Paul's thinking was in *Gezera Shava*! Do you see why it's impossible to understand what he wrote without it? Only through knowing *Gezera Shava* can a person recognize that Paul conflated "those who turn away from God" with "those who use their body parts for the mistreatment of others." To love others is to love God. To mistreat others is to turn away from God. This was the message that Paul conveyed via *Gezera Shava*.

Gezera Shava is an integral part of the New Testament. The New Testament was written within a culture that was thoroughly immersed in it. It truly is impossible to paint an accurate portrait of Paul (or Jesus, for that matter) without it.

Chapter 14

Paul in a Nutshell

Many of Paul's references to keeping the Justices have been lost in translation. Take his discussions on good deeds as an example. The ancient Jewish nation equated "good deeds" (*maasim tovim*) with the Justices—the ethical commandments:

> *Gemilut hasadim* (deeds of mercy) and its nearly synonymous term, ***ma'asim tovim* (good deeds), both refer to those ethical commandments that are considered to be "acts of loving-kindness"**[135]—Karen-Marie Yust (Associate Professor of Christian Education with a Ph.D. from Harvard Divinity School)

These 'deeds of loving-kindness' that are done to fulfill the Justices are mentioned many times in the Greek New Testament. One such place is Acts 9:36:

> Now in Joppa there was a disciple named Tabitha (which translated in Greek is called Dorcas); this woman was abounding with **deeds of kindness** and charity which she continually did.[136]

The Jewish author of Acts was pointing out how dutifully Tabitha kept the Justices through her deeds of kindness and charity. He used a Greek translation of the Hebrew phrase *maasim tovim* in order to do so.[137]

---

135 *Nurturing Child and Adolescent Spirituality: Perspectives from the World's Religious Traditions* by Karen-Marie Yust, p. 277, Rowman & Littlefield, 2006
136 Acts 9:36 NASB
137 The author of Acts used *agatha erga*, (the Greek equivalent of the Hebrew *maasim tovim*)

While the NASB Bible acknowledges the Hebraism in the passage dealing with Tabitha, it fails to acknowledge Paul's derivation of this Hebraism in Romans:

> But because of your stubbornness and unrepentant heart you are storing up wrath for yourself in the day of wrath and revelation of the righteous judgment of God, who WILL RENDER TO EACH PERSON ACCORDING TO HIS DEEDS: **to those who by perseverance in doing good** seek for glory and honor and immortality—eternal life; but **to those who are selfishly ambitious and do not obey the truth, but obey unrighteousness**—wrath and indignation.[138]

The NASB Bible makes it appear that Paul contrasted those who persevere in doing good with those who "obey unrighteousness." However, his message was much more nuanced than that. Paul contrasted those who persevere in deeds of loving kindness with selfish people who treat others unkindly:

> With your meanness and unrepentant heart you are storing up wrath upon yourself for the day of wrath and the revelation of God's equitable judgment. He will "render to every man according to his deeds": **to those who are seeking glory and honor by persevering in deeds of loving kindness**, he will give life in the age to come; but **to those who through selfish ambition have not followed the truth, but instead have followed injustice and unkindness**—there will be wrath and anger.

Paul used the Hebraism to contrast those who fulfill the Justices through deeds of loving kindness with those who don't. He wrote that God's judgment will be based entirely upon that distinction.

Paul's teaching on judgment parallels Jesus'. They both taught that humanity will be divided into two groups. Those who fulfill the Justices by treating others altruistically will receive the reward. The selfish and unjust will be tossed into the fire. However, once again, we find that another of Paul's teachings on altruism has been rewritten as a tirade against moral "unrighteousness" instead.

Modern Bibles mischaracterize Paul through and through. The historical Paul focused on enslavement to the commandment to "Love your neighbor as yourself"—enslavement to the Law of the Messianic King—enslavement to the Justices—enslavement to loving

---

138   Romans 2:5–8 NASB

kindness—enslavement to *dikaiosune*. This was the man who lived during the first century. This was the man who wrote the most books in the New Testament.

Paul in Perspective

Romans Two:

> God will "render to every man according to his deeds": to those who are seeking glory and honor by persevering in deeds of loving-kindness, he will give life in the age to come; but to those who through selfish ambition have not followed the truth, but instead have followed injustice and unkindness—there will be wrath and anger[139]

Romans Three:

> No one's seeking after God. Everyone together avoids him, becoming useless. There isn't anyone showing kindness, not even one. Their throat is an open tomb. They deceive with their tongues. The poison of snakes is under their lips; whose mouth is filled with curses and bitterness. Their feet are eager to shed blood. Destruction and misery lay in their paths. The way of peace they have never known.[140]

Romans Six:

> Do not go on presenting the members of your body to sin as instruments of the unjust, unfair, unkind treatment of others; but present yourselves to God as those alive from the dead, and your members as instruments of just, fair, altruistic treatment of others unto God....[141]

> Having been freed from sin, you've been enslaved to loving kindness.[142]

Romans Thirteen:

> He who loves others has fulfilled the Law because "don't commit adultery," "don't murder," "don't steal," "don't covet," and if there is any other commandment it is summed up in these words: "You shall love your neighbor as yourself."[143]

---

139   Romans 2:6-8
140   Romans 3:11-17
141   Romans 6:13
142   Romans 6:18
143   Romans 13:8-10

Galatians Five:

> You are enslaved to one another through love because the entire Law is fulfilled in one statement, in the precept, "Love your neighbor as yourself."[144]

Galatians Six:

> Bear one another's burdens and thereby fulfill the Law of the Messianic King.[145]

In Paul's pre-Christian days, he strictly adhered to the entire Torah. It was a life-changing event to accept that Jesus had replaced the Torah with the Law of the Messianic King—the precept, "Love your neighbor as yourself." But Paul embraced Jesus 100%. He labored to get others to accept Jesus as the Messianic King, and thereby subject themselves to his Law.

Jesus' Law made morality and ethics very simple: Those who love their neighbors as themselves are following Jesus' Law and everyone else is not. It was truly no more complicated than that. Does this sound like an oversimplification to you? Allow me to demonstrate that this was precisely how Paul understood it.

---

144   Galatians 5:14
145   Galatians 6:2

Chapter 15

Don't Cross the Line

When Jesus declared the Golden Rule to be the entire Law, he drew a hard line in the sand. Paul consistently weighed everything against the Law of the Messianic King to see if it crossed the line. If something violated the Law of the Messianic King, then it was a mortal sin (a sin worthy of spiritual death). If something didn't violate the Law of the Messianic King, then it wasn't a mortal sin. This is easily demonstrated by examining his teachings on jealously, strife, anger, and drunkenness.

Consider jealousy and strife. On one hand, Paul wrote that a person can have some jealousy and strife while remaining in the Messianic King:

> I, too, brothers and sisters, was unable to speak to you as to people of the spirit; instead, I spoke to you as to people of the flesh, **as infants in the Messianic King**. I gave you milk to drink, not solid food: you weren't yet ready; in fact, you're still not ready, because you are still of the flesh. For where **there is jealousy and strife** and division among you, are you not of the flesh, going about like all humans do?[146]

On the other hand, he wrote that anyone who is full of jealousy and strife cannot enter the kingdom of God:

> The works of the flesh are easy to identify: **jealousies… strife…** I'm warning you in advance just as I've warned you about them in advance before, **those who do these things over and over will not inherit the kingdom of God.**[147]

---

146 1 Corinthians 3:1-3 as translated by Dr. William Berg
147 Galatians 5:19-21 as translated by Dr. William Berg

A person who has some jealousy and strife can still generally love their neighbors as themselves. Therefore, they can still be "in the Messianic King." But those who are full of jealousy and strife *have crossed the line*. They violate the Law of the Messianic King. Therefore, they cannot enter the kingdom of God. It's as simple as that.

Consider Paul's teachings on anger as another example. On the one hand, a person can be angry and not even sin:

> **BE ANGRY, AND yet DO NOT SIN**; do not let the sun go down on your anger[148]

On the other hand, a person who is full of anger cannot inherit the kingdom of God:

> The works of the flesh are easy to identify:… **fits of anger**… I'm warning you in advance just as I've warned you about them in advance before, **those who do these things over and over will not inherit the kingdom of God**.[149]

A person can occasionally get angry and still generally love others. But the type of person who is constantly prone to fits of anger *has crossed the line*. He violates the Law of the Messianic King. Therefore, he cannot inherit the kingdom of God. It's as simple as that.

Paul's teachings on drunkenness are yet another example. Paul remarks that getting drunk is dissipation (wasteful extravagance):

> **Do not get drunk with wine, for that is dissipation.**[150]

However, Paul wrote that anyone who continually gets drunk cannot enter the kingdom of God:

> The works of the flesh are easy to identify:… **drunkenness**… I'm warning you in advance just as I've warned you about them in advance before, **those who do these things over and over will not inherit the kingdom of God**.[151]

A person can occasionally get drunk and still generally love others. However, people who live as drunkards don't have the capacity to bear the burdens of others and thereby fulfill the Law of the Messianic

---

148   Ephesians 4:26 NASB
149   Galatians 5:19-21 as translated by Dr. William Berg
150   Ephesians 5:18
151   Galatians 5:19-21 as translated by Dr. William Berg

King. They have *crossed the line*. Having done so, they cannot enter the kingdom of God. It's as simple as that.

Paul is perfectly consistent in his application of the Law of the Messianic King—"Love your neighbor as yourself." Everyone who fulfills this Law is "in the Messianic King," even if their selfish nature hasn't yet been completely eradicated. But, on the other hand, everyone who is full of selfishness *has crossed the line*. They violate the Law of the Messianic King, and so, cannot inherit the kingdom. This is the whole point of Paul's list in Galatians 5:

> The works of the flesh are easy to identify: **sexual immorality**, uncleanliness, no self-control, idolatry, casting love spells,[152] animosity, quarrels, **jealousies, fits of anger, strife**, factions, sects, envy, **drunkenness**, wild parties, and the like; I'm warning you in advance just as I've warned you about them in advance before, **those who do these things over and over** will not inherit the kingdom of God.[153]

Far too often, this list of sins is quoted out of context. Paul composed a list of things that will prevent a person from entering the kingdom of God *if, and only if, a person's entire life is consumed by them.*

Notice that Paul included sexual immorality as part of this critical distinction. Notice that he treated sexual immorality in the very same way as jealousy, strife, anger, and drunkenness. Why in the world did he do this? Well, he had to. The Law of the Messianic King required it.

---

152   Paul's word here is *pharmakeia*, "the use of charms" (devices or spells). The Greek bucolic poet Theocritus, in his well-known second Idyll (entitled *Pharmakeutria*) portrays a love-lorn sorceress employing both to regain her lover. The Koine papyri discovered in Egypt show that the vast majority of spells cast were designed to win someone's sexual interest.
153   Galatians 5:19-21 as translated by Dr. William Berg

Chapter 16

Separation Anxiety

Paul weighed everything against the Law of the Messianic King—
"Love your neighbor as yourself." He even weighed sexual acts against
Leviticus 19:18. Here is Paul's most striking example of this:

Engagement in dishonorable passions incurred a <u>bodily</u> penalty for the error.

> On account of this, **God handed them over to <u>dishonorable</u>**
> **passions.** For both their females exchanged instinctual function
> for one contrary to instinct. And in the same way, indeed, the
> males exchanged the instinctual use of the female burning away
> in their lust for one another—males with males—resulting in
> disgraceful acts, **and they <u>received in themselves the full penalty</u>**
> **necessary for their error.**

Engagement in unallowable things incurred a <u>spiritual</u> penalty for the error.

> And as they tried not to prove the things of God via examination,
> **God handed them over to a worthless mind to do <u>unallowable</u>**
> **things:** full of every injustice, worthlessness, greed, and
> maliciousness; full of envy, discord, deceit, meanspiritedness, and
> rumors; they speak bad of others and abhor the existence of God;
> they insult, proudly brag, invent ways to inflict physical pain and
> disobey their parents; they are untrustworthy and they break their
> contracts.
>
> They are heartless, hostile and unmerciful. And they recognize
> **God's requirement of justice (that <u>those who spend their time</u>**
> **<u>this way deserve death</u>)**[154]

---

154   Romans 1:26-32

Paul specified that "dishonorable passions" and "unallowable things" result in different consequences. The "dishonorable passions" result in a *bodily* penalty while the "unallowable things" result in a *spiritual* penalty. Only the unallowable things were sins worthy of spiritual death:

> **Even though Paul includes what we call homosexual behavior within his list of symptoms of human rebellion, it is evident that he hardly regards it as the most serious even of those.** The climax of his discussion of the results of human rebellion against God is, as we have noted, the list of "cold" sins, sins of "strength," in 1.28-31–**"murder, strife, deceit, malignity, vicious gossips, public slanderers, haters of God, insolent, haughty, boasters, inventors of evil…faithless, heartless, ruthless."** These he sees as the most destructive sins, and **it is only of these that he says those who commit them are "worthy of death"** (1.32).[155]—Christopher Bryan (C. K. Benedict Professor of New Testament at The University of the South)

It is quite bewildering that conservative Christians quote Romans 1 as their primary proof against homosexuality. This chapter happens to be one of the most liberal passages in the entire Bible.

In Paul's theology, the same-sex acts described in Romans 1 aren't worthy of spiritual death. Those who engaged in them didn't cross the line.

Paul separated the homosexual acts from the sins worthy of spiritual death. Yet modern Christians somehow claim that Romans condemns homosexuals to hell. They have missed Paul's purposeful separation based on the Law of the Messianic King.

Things become even more interesting when we realize that the homosexual acts in Romans 1 *were related to idolatry*:

> They transformed the glory of an incorruptible God into the likeness of a corruptible human, or of winged things or quadrupeds or serpents. That is why God has let them pass over, amid their hearts' wild desires, to the unclean act of dishonoring their bodies—those, that is, who perverted God's truth with a lie, and **revered and worshipped the creation instead of the creator**, the creator who is blessed into the ages to come, Amen. **That is why God has let them pass over into dishonorable passions.**[156]

---

155   *A Preface to Romans: Notes on the Epistle in its Literary and Cultural Setting*, by Christopher Bryan, p.88, Oxford University Press, USA (June 15, 2000)
156   Romans 1:23-25

Paul wrote about dishonorable homosexual passions which arose from idolatry. On the surface, this appears to make matters even more confusing. After all, shouldn't *idolatrous* homosexual acts qualify as sins worthy of spiritual death? Surprisingly, it's the opposite. The specific idolatrous acts that Paul was referring to couldn't be labeled as "sins worthy of spiritual death." Why not? The historical reason for this is the topic of the following chapter.

Chapter 17
Gay Old Time

Paul wrote his letter to the Romans while in Corinth, or very shortly after staying there:

> Paul spent three months in Greece (primarily Corinth; cf Ac 20:2-3), during which time he wrote Romans.[157]—Tremper Longman (Robert H. Gundry Professor of Biblical Studies at Westmont College)

The pagan mystery religion of Bacchus-Dionysus was popular in Corinth:

> Dionysus/Bacchus was popular in Corinth.[158]—Khiok-Khng Yeo (Harry R. Kendall Professor of New Testament at Garrett-Evangelical Theological Seminary)

* * *

> By the time of the apostle Paul, the cult of Dionysus or Bacchus was well established in most of the major cities in which Paul preached.[159]—Roy B. Zuck (Dr. Zuck was awarded the 2009 Warren S. Benson distinguished Educator award by the North American Professors of Christian Education.)

Pausanias, a second-century geographer, witnessed two statues of Bacchus-Dionysus during his visit to Corinth.[160] These statues were

---

157 *Romans-Galatians* by Tremper Longman, David E. Garland, p. 418, Zondervan, 2008
158 *Rhetorical Interaction in 1 Corinthians 8 and 10: A Formal Analysis with Preliminary Suggestions for a Chinese, Cross-cultural Hermeneutic* by Khiok-Khng Yeo, p. 107, BRILL, 1995
159 *Vital New Testament Issues: Examining New Testament Passages and Problems* by Roy B. Zuck, p. 166, Kregel Academic, 1996
160 Pausanias, Description of Greece 2.2

likely seen by Paul, as well.[161]

The activities of mystery religions were generally kept secret. However, a scandal that broke out in 186 BCE made the Bacchus-Dionysus initiation rites public knowledge. The ancient historian Livy records that initiation into Bacchus Dionysus involved a homosexual orgy:

> The Roman Livy (59 B.C.—A.D. 17) testifies of the homosexuality and other debauchery involved in the worship of Bacchic Dionysus.—James B. DeYoung (Professor of New Testament Literature and Language at Western Seminary)

> * * *

> Dionysian mysteries were connected with male-homosexual initiation rites[162]—David F. Greenberg (Professor of Sociology at New York University)

Livy's works were popular in Paul's day. In fact, Livy was still alive during Paul's earliest childhood years. Also, numerous scholars point to the possibility of a direct connection between Paul's metaphor in Romans 12 and the one used by Livy:[163]

> In Romans 12:4-5 Paul employs the metaphor of the one body and its many members to refer to the right relationship among Christians in Rome. Livy has Menenius Agrippa use the same metaphor to advocate unity when the plebs rebelled (Livy 2.3.21).[164]—Anthony J. Guerra (Associate Professor of Humanities at University of Bridgeport)

Livy's writings would have informed Paul about the Bacchus-Dionysus homosexual orgy initiations. Such a vivid practice must have crossed his mind each time he saw a Bacchus-Dionysus statue or walked by one of the Bacchic temples in Greece. Naturally, Paul must have been less than thrilled at the thought of those idolatrous homosexual orgies. So he railed against them in Romans 1.

---

161   The names Bacchus and Dionysus both refer to the same god and mystery religion. The ancient Greeks used both names; "Dionysus" is more or less Greek, and may allude to his origin as "offspring of Zeus," while "Bacchus," a non-Greek (Lydian) word, may have pointed to his origins in "the mysterious east." For simplicity's sake, I will refer to this mystery religion as that of Bacchus-Dionysus throughout.

162   *The Construction of Homosexuality* by David F. Greenberg, p. 154, University of Chicago Press, 1990

163   Scholars who equate Paul's and Livy's metaphors also include Klaus Haacker and Margaret M. Mitchell among others.

164   *Romans and the Apologetic Tradition: The Purpose, Genre, and Audience of Paul's Letter* by Anthony J. Guerra p. 159, Cambridge University Press, 1995

But doesn't the fact that they were *orgies* also qualify them as sins worthy of spiritual death? Wouldn't the mixture of orgies plus idolatry plus same-sex intercourse be a sin worthy of spiritual death? Not according to Romans 1. But how in the world can this be? The short answer is: The participants were under the age of twenty.

> the initiation was performed on three set days in the year, before being **available five times a month for men** (ibid., 13, 8-9), **preferably the under-twenties** (ibid., 10, 16).[165]—Robert Turcan (Professor of Roman History at the Sorbonne)

* * *

> To be sure, an important factor in the [Bacchus Dionysus] scandal was the sexual excess thought to characterize the Bacchic rites, and **this included the sexual initiation of young men under the age of twenty**.[166]—Craig Arthur Williams (Associate Professor of Classics at Brooklyn College)

According to Judith Evans Grubbs, Professor of Roman History, the marrying age of young Romans centered on the age of twenty.[167] Therefore, the idolatrous homosexual orgies of 186 BCE primarily involved unmarried young adults. These unmarried folks weren't committing adultery. They weren't violating any of the Justices. Therefore, when it came to the Law of the Messianic King, *they weren't crossing the line.* As long as the acts were committed by single people, Paul didn't have the leeway to label them "sins worthy of spiritual death." He couldn't and he didn't.

It is also possible that Paul was referring not to the sexual practices of Bacchic initiates in his distant past, but to the sexual practices of the priests and priestesses of a variety of goddess cults that were popular during Paul's day. In his paper, "Paul, the Goddess Religions and Queers: Romans 1:23-28," Jeramy Townsley demonstrates how the sexual practices of the unmarried priests and priestesses of various goddess cults likewise fulfill Paul's depiction:

165   *The Gods of Ancient Rome: Religion in Everyday Life from Archaic to Imperial Times* by Robert Turcan, p. 118, Taylor & Francis, 2001

166   *Roman Homosexuality: Ideologies of Masculinity in Classical Antiquity* by Craig Arthur Williams, p. 111, Oxford University Press US, 1999

167   *Women and the Law in the Roman Empire: A Sourcebook on Marriage, Divorce and Widowhood* by Judith Evans Grubbs, p. 88, Psychology Press, 2002

the entire context of Romans 1:23-28 is about idolatry, and the sexual references specifically oriented the original reader to the sacred sex practices of the goddess cults.... That Paul would have been familiar with goddess religions seems inescapable. Temples and shrines to Cybele, Artemis, Venus/Aphrodite, Astarte, and others were scattered densely around the region of Paul's upbringing and missionary travels (Asia Minor, Greece, Cyprus, etc.)—Jeramy Townsley (adjunct faculty member in sociology at Butler University)[168]

Was Paul speaking of the unmarried initiates into Bacchus-Dionysus? Was he addressing the unmarried priests and priestesses of other goddess cults? Was he addressing another idolatrous homosexual orgy practice that has been lost to the historical record? It does not matter. In any case:

> ***Romans 1 addresses an idolatrous homosexual orgy practice that Paul purposefully excluded from the sins worthy of spiritual death.***

That much the passage makes abundantly clear.

Even when faced with orgies plus idolatry plus homosexuality, the Law of the Messianic King was Paul's acid test for determining what constituted mortal sin and what did not. Romans 1 documents this in a very dramatic way. The historical Paul was extremely different from the mythical Paul invented by religious institutions.

---

168   "Paul, the Goddess Religions and Queers: Romans 1:23-28" by Jeramy Townsley, 2002

Chapter 18

Idol Hands

Most Christians assume that the apostle Paul condemned all forms of idolatry. Yet, surprisingly, he didn't. In fact, Paul even chided Christians who judged others for eating meat that had been sacrificed to idols:

> Eat anything that is sold in the meat market without asking questions for conscience' sake; FOR THE EARTH IS THE LORD'S, AND ALL IT CONTAINS. **If one of the unbelievers invites you and you want to go, eat anything that is set before you without asking questions for conscience' sake.**

> But if anyone says to you, "This is meat sacrificed to idols," do not eat it, for the sake of the one who informed you, and for conscience' sake; **I mean not your own conscience, but the other man's; for why is my freedom judged by another's conscience? If I partake with thankfulness, why am I slandered concerning that for which I give thanks?**[169]

When it came to eating meat that had been sacrificed to idols, Paul had a "Don't ask, don't tell" policy. He even said that Christians bothered by meat sacrificed to idols were wrongly "slandering" those who knew that it's okay. He rebuked the Christians who judged others for eating idolatrous meat.

We've now encountered two instances in which Paul did not consider idolatrous practices to be sins worthy of spiritual death.

---

169   1 Corinthians 10:24–30 NASB

- Paul separated the pre-marital idolatrous homosexual orgies from sins that lead to death. (Although he still forbade it because of other, non-spiritual penalties.)

- Paul told the Corinthians that eating meat sacrificed to idols was another idolatrous practice that does not lead to spiritual death. In this instance, Paul even says to go for it, provided it doesn't harm the faith of the spiritually immature.

At all times, Paul applied the Law of the Messianic King to determine what constitutes sin that leads to death and what does not, even when it came to idolatry, and even when it came to idolatry and sex combined.

Chapter 19

Jerusalem Council

It is fascinating that Paul chided those who judged others for eating meat that had been sacrificed to idols. This is especially fascinating when we realize that the Jerusalem Council commanded Christians to *abstain* from eating meat sacrificed to idols:

> **For it seemed good to the Holy Spirit** and to us to lay upon you no greater burden than these essentials: **that you *abstain* from things sacrificed to idols** and from blood and from things strangled and from fornication; if you keep yourselves free from such things, you will do well.[170]

Paul's "Don't ask, don't tell" policy guaranteed that his converts would imbibe a lot of meat that had been sacrificed to idols. They certainly were not "*abstaining* from things sacrificed to idols." So was Paul teaching his converts to disobey a commandment from "the Holy Spirit" himself?

There is no doubt that Paul taught his converts to violate *the letter of the Law*. The letter of the Law demanded abstinence, pure and simple. Paul, however, understood *the spirit of the Law*. He understood the Law's intention. The Jerusalem Council issued the commandment in order to appease some Pharisees who had become Christians:

> Some men came down from Judea and began teaching the brethren, "Unless you are circumcised according to the custom of Moses, you cannot be saved." And when Paul and Barnabas had great dissension and debate with them, the brethren determined that Paul and Barnabas and some others of

---

170   Acts 15:28–29 NASB

them should go up to Jerusalem to the apostles and elders concerning this issue.

Therefore, being sent on their way by the church, they were passing through both Phoenicia and Samaria, describing in detail the conversion of the Gentiles, and were bringing great joy to all the brethren. When they arrived at Jerusalem, they were received by the church and the apostles and the elders, and they reported all that God had done with them.

But some of the sect of the Pharisees who had believed stood up, saying, "It is necessary to circumcise them and to direct them to observe the Law of Moses."[171]

It was during this debate on "observing the Law of Moses" that the Jerusalem Council decided to impose the prohibition on eating meat that had been sacrificed to idols. It was a compromise to appease certain Christian Pharisees.

Many Christian Pharisees refused to associate with anyone who ate idolatrous meat. So the council (and the Holy Spirit) decided that it was better for converts not to eat idol meat *when it would offend another Christian brother.* Paul understood the intention of the commandment, and so he taught it to his converts:

But it is not what we eat that will put us on God's side. We don't fall behind if we don't eat it, and we don't get ahead if we do eat it. See to it, though, that your own exercise of freedom does not become an obstacle to the unsteady. For if they see you, who have knowledge, reclining at table in a phantom god's temple, won't they, with their unsteady feelings, be encouraged toward the practice of eating sacrificial meat?

In your display of knowledge, the unsteady one has been lost, the brother or sister for whom the Messianic King died. By sinning against your brothers and sisters and assaulting their unsteady feelings, you are sinning against the Messianic King.

That's why if what I eat offends my brother or sister, let me not dream of eating meat from here to eternity, so as not to offend my brother or sister.[172]

When it came to secretly eating meat that had been sacrificed

---

171   Acts 15:1–5 NASB
172   1 Corinthians 8:8-13 as translated by Dr. William Berg

to idols, Paul said, "Go for it!" But if it "offended a brother or sister," then it became a "sin against the Messianic King." Paul taught the *intention* of the Jerusalem Council's commandment, not the *letter* of it.

The Jerusalem Council's commandments illustrate the danger of the "God said it; I believe it; and that settles it for me" mentality. Such an absolutist mindset often allows the letter of the Law to obscure the spirit of the Law. Paul didn't say, "God said abstain from idol meat; I believe it, and that settles it for me." On the contrary, he sought to understand *why* it was commanded. While his final analysis allowed his followers to eat idol meat, he still commanded them to *fulfill the intention of the command*. He commanded them not to eat the meat when it would offend an immature Christian brother or sister.

The only area where Paul had a "God said it; I believe it; and that settles it for me" mindset is when it came to the Law of the Messianic King. Modern Christians would do well to follow Paul's lead on this. "God said that 'Love your neighbor as yourself' is the entire Law; I believe it; and that settles it for me." That mindset would align the modern Christian 100% with the thinking and theology of the historical Paul. Paul's interpretation of the Jerusalem Council's commandments shows this to be so.

Chapter 20

Just a Suggestion

Paul would fear for his own soul if he taught anything against the Law of the Messianic King. Therefore, he had to tread lightly when his converts did something he abhorred, yet weren't violating the Law of the Messianic King.

For example, not only were his Corinthian converts eating idolatrous meat, but they were even dining in pagan temples! So, did Paul tell them, "God commands you to stop participating in pagan ceremonies"? No. He couldn't and he didn't. Because they weren't violating the Law of the Messianic King, he had to employ a different tactic with them:

> Therefore, my beloved, **turn away from idolatry**. I'm speaking to intelligent people; **make up your own minds about what I say**.
>
> The Cup of Blessing that we bless—is it not a partaking in the blood of the Messianic King? The bread that we break—is it not a partaking in the body of the Messianic King? Since it is one loaf, we are many in one body, for all of us share in the one loaf.
>
> Look at the descendants of Israel: are not those who eat the sacrifices also partaking in the sacrificial table? **So what am I saying**? That there is any significance in sacrificial meat? Or that there is any significance in an idol? No, but what they sacrifice, they sacrifice to godlets and not to God, and **I'm not willing to let you be partakers in godlets**. You can't drink both the Master's cup and the godlets' cup. You can't share both the Master's table and the godlets' table. Or are we trying to provoke the Master to jealousy?

Do we think we're stronger than him?[173]

Paul took the opposite of the "thus sayeth the Lord" approach. He took the "thus sayeth *Paul* approach" instead. He even gave his audience room to reject what *he* was saying. Over and over again, he reminded his readers that *he* didn't want them to participate in the pagan ceremonies:

> make up your own minds about what I say.

* * *

> So what am I saying?

* * *

> I'm not willing to let you be partakers in godlets

"I say." "I say." "I'm not willing." "Make up your own mind about it." This was Paul's approach to yet another form of idolatry.

Dr. Tom Wright observed Paul's cautious, guarded tone:

> **Paul seems to be arguing this somewhat cautiously**, because he says in verse 15 that they will need to think through what he's saying.[174]—N.T. Wright (N.T. Wright is one of the world's leading New Testament scholars. In addition to his doctorate from Oxford University, he also has been awarded several honorary doctoral degrees, including from St. Andrews University [2009], John Leland Center for Theological Studies [2008], Durham University [2007], Wycliffe College [2006], Gordon College [2003] and Aberdeen University [2001]. N.T. Wright was also awarded honorary fellowship at Merton College [2004] and Downing College [2003].)

We learn a lot about the historical Paul when we contrast the mortal sins in Romans 1 with his various teachings on idolatry:

---

173   1 Corinthians 10:14-22 as translated by Dr. William Berg
174   *Paul for Everyone: 1 Corinthians* by Tom Wright, Westminster John Knox Press, 2004, p. 130

- Paul unabashedly wrote to the Romans that arrogant people deserve spiritual death. Yet he told the Corinthians that those participating in pagan temples should "make up their own minds" about whether or not to stop. Arrogance was condemned in the strongest possible terms. Participating in pagan ceremonies was a different matter altogether.

- Paul unabashedly wrote to the Romans that those who spread rumors deserve spiritual death. Yet he told his converts to not worry about eating meat sacrificed to idols. Rumor-mongering was condemned in the strongest possible terms. Eating idolatrous meat was a different matter altogether.

- Paul unabashedly wrote to the Romans that those who speak badly of others deserve spiritual death. Yet he separated idolatrous homosexual orgies from the sins worthy of spiritual death. Bad-mouthing others was condemned in the strongest possible terms. Participating in idolatrous homosexual orgies was a different matter altogether.

The arrogant, the rumor-mongers, and those who bad-mouthed others all violate the Law of the Messianic King. When it came to violations of the Law of the Messianic King, Paul unabashedly categorized them as sins worthy of spiritual death. But when it came to non-violations of the Law of the Messianic King, even non-violations involving idolatry, Paul refused to label them as sins worthy of spiritual death. For Paul, arrogant people, those who spread rumors, and those who speak badly of others are far worse than:

- Those who ate idol meat.

- Those who participated in pagan temples.

- Those who engaged in idolatrous homosexual orgy practices.

The world needs to understand the values of the historical Paul. His values were extremely different from those of the mythical Paul promoted by modern religious institutions.

Chapter 21

Living in a Material World

There were a lot of idolatrous practices that Paul abhorred, yet he wouldn't label as sins worthy of spiritual death. So is this it? Was there any form of idolatry that Paul considered to be a sin worthy of spiritual death? Yes, there was:

> No greedy person—such a man is an idolater—has an inheritance in the kingdom of the Messianic King and God.—Ephesians 5:5

In the Pauline school of thought, greed is the form of idolatry that prevents a person from entering the kingdom of God. But where did Paul get the idea that *greed is idolatry*? For one thing, he got the idea from Jesus:

> No one can serve two masters; for either he will hate the one and love the other, or he will be devoted to one and despise the other. You cannot serve God and wealth.[175]—Jesus

In Jesus' famous Sermon on the Mount, he declared that those who serve wealth cannot serve God. In other words, greed is idolatry.

This concept of greed as idolatry happened to be a popular first-century Jewish notion. For example, Philo, a Jewish contemporary of Paul, wrote:

> Moses says, in another passage, "You shall not follow images, and you shall not make to yourselves molten Gods." Teaching them, by figurative language, that **it is not right to pay such honors to wealth as one would**

175   Matthew 6:24 NASB

78

pay to the gods; for those celebrated materials of wealth, silver and gold, are made to be used, which, however, the multitude follows, looking upon them as the only causes of wealth which is proverbially called blind, and the especial sources of happiness. **These are the things which Moses calls idols**[176]—Philo

Jesus, Paul and Philo (a non-Christian Jew) all considered greed to be idolatry. Some ancient rabbis even considered any neglect of charity to be idolatry too:

> Certain rabbis considered the neglect of charity to be tantamount to idolatry for very much the same reason (*t. Pe'ah* 4:20; *b. Ketub.* 68a; *B. Bat.* 10a; *Sipre Deut.* 117).—Christopher Hays (D. Wilson Moore Assistant Professor of Ancient Near Eastern Studies at Fuller Theological Seminary)[177]

The idea that greed is idolatry was an established first-century notion. Under the Law of the Messianic King—"Love your neighbor as yourself"—it was only natural for Paul to consider this to be the one form of idolatry that prevents a person from entering God's kingdom.

> No greedy person — such a man is an idolater — has an inheritance in the kingdom of the Messianic King and God.—Ephesians 5:5

It's worth noting that the Pauline school of thought equates greed with idolatry twice in the New Testament—once in Ephesians (see above) and once in Colossians as well:

> greed, which is idolatry—Colossians 3:5

Paul's writings are perfectly consistent. The Law of the Messianic King was his simple divining rod. Any form of idolatry that violates Leviticus 19:18 is mortal sin; greed is an example of this. Any form of idolatry that doesn't violate Leviticus 19:18 isn't mortal sin; idolatrous homosexual orgy fests are an example of this.

That's the historical Paul.

---

176   Philo, Special Laws 1.24
177   *Luke's Wealth Ethics: A Study in Their Coherence and Character* by Christopher Hays, p. 34, Mohr Siebeck, 2010

Chapter 22
Mystery Solved

It was in Romans 1 that Paul separated pre-marital, idolatrous, homosexual orgies from sins worthy of spiritual death. Romans 1 set the stage for the next chapter, Romans 2. Paul's contrast of "pre-marital homosexual orgies" to "sins worthy of spiritual death" set the stage for him to declare:

> **The doers of the Torah are those who will be vindicated.**—Romans 2:13

In Romans 2:13, Paul wrote that only those who follow the Torah (Moses' Law) will be vindicated before God. Say what? Doesn't this statement contradict everything else he wrote? This statement has troubled religious commentators for centuries:

> **Paul's statements about the law sometimes seem to contradict one another.** As an example, Paul in Romans 3:20 stated that no one can be declared righteous by observing the law, whereas Romans 2:13 seems to state just the opposite.... **The debate on Paul's view of the law is far from finished and promises to continue for a long time to come.**—John B. Polhill (professor of New Testament at Southern Baptist Theological Seminary. He is the author of the Acts volume in the New American Commentary.)[178]

Since the beginning of the Christian Church, no scholar (either Catholic or Protestant) has put forth a definitive reconciliation of Romans 1–3. (Not a single commentator has proposed a solution that accounts for *every single verse* within these three chapters.):

---

178   *Paul and His Letters* by John B. Polhill, pp. 296-297, B&H Publishing Group, 1999

The interpretation of Romans 1:18-3:20 has been notoriously difficult for almost every commentator. Problems begin to take form when one attempts to identify exactly who is being talked about or addressed in the passage…. **Earlier interpreters such as Origen, Jerome, Augustine, and Erasmus wrestled with this issue, and it continues to plague commentators today….**

No one being able to be declared righteous by observing the law (Romans 3:20) is clear, [yet] there are four texts in Romans 2 that seem to espouse a theology of salvation by works or by obedience to the Mosaic Law.[179]— Richard N. Longenecker (Distinguished Professor of New Testament B.A., M.A. Wheaton College; Ph.D. New College, University of Edinburgh)

As a cryptographer, I've always been intrigued by unsolved puzzles. I built a successful career out of solving the 'unsolvable.' Now, I'm pleased to present **the definitive solution that has eluded theologians for almost 2,000 years.** How do I know that Romans 1–3 is definitively solved? Simple: *the solution allows for every sentence in the passage to be held true without contradiction* for the first time in two thousand years. I have discovered the simple, straightforward, direct, historical answer.

Did Paul write that only the doers of the Torah will be vindicated before God? Yes, he did. Then he proceeded to explain *exactly* who is a doer of the Torah and who is a violator of it. His description is fascinating:

The doers of the Torah are those who will be vindicated.

For example, **when gentiles who don't have the Torah do naturally what the Torah requires, those gentiles without the Torah are the Torah unto themselves. They are demonstrating the performance of the law written on their hearts,** with their conscience testifying for them and their thoughts alternately either accusing or defending them on that day when God judges people's secrets, according to the gospel that I have, through the Messianic King Jesus.

But if you call yourself a Jew and rest your hopes upon Torah and speak loudly of God and know his will and assent to the provisions of Torah that really make a difference, and you're determined to be a guide for the blind, a light for those in the dark, a mentor for the foolish, a pedagogue for children, trained in the knowledge and truth in Torah — so you're teaching

179   *Studies in Paul, exegetical and theological by Richard N. Longenecker*, p. 98, Sheffield Phoenix Press, 2004

another, and you're not teaching yourself?

You're preaching not to steal, and you're stealing! You're saying not to commit adultery, and you're committing adultery! Idols disgust you, but you plunder their temples! You speak loudly of Torah, but bring dishonor on God by breaking the Torah! "Thanks to you, the name of God is being profaned among the heathen," just as it is written.

Circumcision is a good thing, if you keep the Torah; but **if you become a violator of the Torah, your circumcision has turned into a foreskin. So if the uncircumcised keeps the Justices of the Torah,**[180] **won't his foreskin be reckoned as circumcision?** And the one who is from birth uncircumcised, and who accomplishes the Torah—won't he be the one to judge you, a violator of the law though you have its letter and your circumcision?[181]

This passage is actually easy to understand now that you've been taught about the Justices and the Jobs. The passage discusses two groups of people:

- Gentiles who instinctively keep the Justices of the Torah, but do not even know about the Jobs.

- Jews who keep the Jobs of the Torah while they are violating the Justices.

The Christian Jews were circumcised and boasted of keeping the Jobs of the Torah. Meanwhile, they were stealing, committing adultery, and plundering temples. They were violating the Justices of the Torah. Paul's message to them is simple:

- If you keep the Jobs but violate the Justices, God will treat you as if you didn't keep the Jobs. ("Your circumcision has turned into a foreskin.") In other words, **if you violate the Justices, you will be considered to be a violator of the entire Torah.**

- If you keep the Justices but violate the Jobs, then God will treat you as if you kept the Jobs. ("If the uncircumcised

---

180   See the next chapter, "Oxymoron," for documentation regarding the translation "Justices of the Torah."

181   Romans 2:12-27 as translated by Dr. William Berg. Most translations have question marks for Romans 2:21-23. However, the lack of interrogative particles in the Greek indicates a series of exclamations rather than questions.

observes the Justices of the Torah, won't his foreskin be reckoned as circumcision?") In other words, **if you keep the Justices, you will be considered to have kept the entire Torah.**

Paul starts by saying that only the doers of the Torah will be vindicated before God. Then he explains that anyone who keeps the Justices will be considered to have kept the entire Torah. They are the doers of the entire Torah, who are vindicated before God. It's just that easy.

So now let's take a look at what he communicated in Romans 2:13-26 and 3:20:

The doers of the Justices of the Torah will be vindicated.

∗ ∗ ∗

By the Jobs of the Torah, no one will be vindicated.

There's no contradiction at all. There really was nothing for commentators to bellyache over for centuries. After all, both passages say the very same thing. They are two sides of the same coin! Romans 2 teaches that only the doers of the Justices will be vindicated before God. Romans 3 teaches that no one will be vindicated by the Jobs. They are two ways of saying exactly the same thing. There's nothing to even resolve.

Now that we've connected Romans 2 and 3, how does Romans 1 serve as a setup? Paul wrote in Romans 2 that those who violate the Justices are guilty of breaking the entire Law. This is why those who speak badly of others, those who spread rumors, those who are arrogant, etc. are committing sins worthy of spiritual death. They are violating the Justices and guilty of breaking the entire Law.

On the other hand, Paul wrote that anyone who keeps the Justices will be considered to have kept the entire Law. If those engaged in pre-marital, idolatrous, homosexual orgies keep the Justices, then they will be considered to have kept the entire Law. That's why Paul didn't label this activity as a sin worthy of spiritual death.

Modern Christianity now has a dilemma. All the pieces of Romans 1–3 have been seamlessly put together for the first time in 2,000 years. The historical puzzle is completely solved. What are Christians going to do with this information?

Chapter 23

Oxymoron

So why don't Christians know that Romans 1–3 is contrasting the Jobs to the Justices? There's actually a very straightforward answer. In modern Bibles, it's literally impossible to see the contrast since the contrast has been removed.

Allow me to demonstrate. Here is a literal translation of Romans 2:26 from the original Greek:

> If the uncircumcised keeps the Justices of the Torah, won't his foreskin be reckoned as circumcision?

The Justices of the Torah are the key to the Great Romans Paradox. With this in mind, try to find 'the Justices of the Torah' in modern translations of Romans 2:26:

> if an uncircumcised man keeps **the precepts of the law**, will he not be considered circumcised?—Romans 2:26 NAB

* * *

> if those who are not circumcised keep **the law's requirements**, will they not be regarded as though they were circumcised?—Romans 2:26 NIV

* * *

> if the uncircumcised man keeps **the requirements of the Law**, will not his uncircumcision be regarded as circumcision?—Romans 2:26 NASB

Modern translations claim that Paul wrote about an uncircumcised man who keeps all the precepts of Moses' Law. Aside from being mistranslated, it's also self-contradictory. An uncircumcised man cannot keep all the requirements of a law that requires circumcision! Yet all modern Bibles use such an oxymoronic sentence in Romans 2:26.

The most learned Greek scholar of the entire Byzantine Age tried to get Christians to steer clear of that oxymoron. Who was this man? His name was Photius:

Photius became the most versatile scholar of his age—*Who's Who in Christian History*[182]

* * *

Perhaps the most famous figure from this period was Photius, Patriarch at Constantinople twice late in the ninth century, a strong opponent of Iconoclasm, and the greatest scholar of his time.[183]—Thomas M. Conley (PhD in Greek Literature and participating faculty member in Medieval Studies at University of Illinois)

* * *

Photius, arguably Byzantium's greatest intellect—Michael McCormick (Francis Goelet Professor of Medieval History at Harvard University)[184]

* * *

The greatest polymath of the age was Photius—Warren T. Treadgold (NEH Professor of Byzantine Studies)[185]

A polymath is "a person of great learning in several fields of study."[186] Such was Photius, the greatest scholar of the entire Byzantine Age. Photius' native language was Greek. He had a particular passion

---

182   *Who's Who in Christian History* by J. D. Douglas, Philip Wesley Comfort, p. 564, Tyndale House Publishers, Inc., 1992

183   *Rhetoric in the European Tradition* by Thomas M. Conley, p. 66, University of Chicago Press, 1994

184   *Origins of the European economy: Communications and Commerce, A.D. 300-900, Parts 300-900* by Michael McCormick, p. 182, Cambridge University Press, 2001

185   *A History of the Byzantine State and Society* by Warren T. Treadgold, p. 562, Stanford University Press, 1997

186   "polymath." Dictionary.com Unabridged. Random House, Inc. 25 Aug. 2011. <Dictionary.com http://dictionary.reference.com/browse/polymath>.

for ancient Greek. He even compiled a lexicon to study the differences between ancient and Byzantine Greek, a lexicon that is still referenced to this day:

> It contains the text of a ninth-century Greek lexicon compiled by Photius, Patriarch of Constantinople. The lexicon was a tool for Byzantine Greeks studying the works of ancient authors, whose language and vocabulary differed significantly from the day-to-day language spoken in the Byzantine Empire. The lexicon offers the modern scholar a wealth of information regarding ancient works that Photius had access to but are no longer extant.[187]

Photius understood the fluidity of language. He understood that Paul's usage of language was rooted in the peculiarities of first-century Greek. When reading Romans 2:26 in its original language, Photius understood it as follows:

> If the uncircumcised keeps the Torah's Code of Justice, won't his foreskin be reckoned as circumcision?—Translated by Dr. William Berg (formerly Professor of Classical Studies at UCLA, Stanford, 'Atenisi University and St. John's College, and author of a wide range of publications on classical antiquity)

Photius understood that Romans 2:26 wasn't discussing *the entire Law*. He understood that that would be an oxymoron. He understood that Romans 2:26 was referring to a specific group of commandments. Here's Photius in his own words:

> (Commentary on Romans 2:26) "So if the uncircumcised observes the Justices of the Torah": he doesn't say "observes the Torah," lest the Jew say, "And **how is it possible for an uncircumcised person to observe the Torah when he's transgressing the Torah on that very issue, the fact of being uncircumcised?**" Therefore, so as not to give those people a handle on that issue, he doesn't put it that way. Instead, he says "the Justices of the Torah." For the Jews, he talks about "the Torah;" **for the uncircumcised, he talks about "the Justices of the Torah." He is saying, "I didn't speak of the whole law, but only of the justice-related parts ..."**—Photius (as translated by Dr. William Berg)

The greatest scholar of the Byzantine Age tried to awaken Christians to the fact that Paul was referring to a distinct group of

---

187   *Photiou Tou Patriarchou Lexeon Synagoge: E Codice Galeano Descripsit* by Ricardus Porsonus (Richard Porson's renowned 1822 edition of Photius), edited by Peter Paul Dobree, Introductory Page, Cambridge University Press, 2010

commandments in Romans 2:26, not the entire Law. Modern translators not only ignore the pleas of one of the greatest language scholars of all time, but they stubbornly insist on writing a self-contradictory sentence instead. It's one thing to choose to ignore scholarship. It's quite another to insist upon a self-contradictory translation when doing so.

The translators almost appear to be deliberately concealing the fact that Paul contrasted the Justices of the Torah (in Romans 2) to the Jobs of the Torah (in Romans 3). Sadly, the foundational premise of Romans has been lost in translation. The rest of the letter, which fully rests on this premise, gets terribly misconstrued, including Paul's discussion on homosexuality.

Paul's letter was based on the premise that anyone who keeps the Justices of the Torah is a doer of the Law, and therefore, vindicated before God. Every thought in Romans 1:26-3:20 is built upon this premise:

- Since participants in pre-marital, idolatrous, homosexual orgies aren't violating the Justices, they are not committing a sin worthy of spiritual death.—Romans 1:26-27

- However, those who speak badly of others, those who spread rumors, and those who are arrogant do violate the Justices, and therefore, are committing sins worthy of spiritual death—Romans 1:28-32

- Since the Justices are all that matter, God will impartially judge all humanity according to their persistence in deeds of loving kindness —Romans 2:1-11

- The doers of the Justices are considered to have kept the entire law, and they are vindicated before God for doing so—Romans 2:12-29

- Jobs (such as circumcision) don't cover over violations of the Justices (such as injustice, lying, and malice)—Romans 3:1-8

- Those who use their body parts for the unjust treatment of others are violating the Justices, and therefore, are rejecting God himself.—Romans 3:9-18

- By the Jobs of the Torah no one will be vindicated in God's sight, for through the Law's Justices comes the knowledge of sin—Romans 3:19-20

There you have it—the entire passage that had mystified scholars for 2,000 years. Knowing the Justices and Jobs makes the passage very easy to understand. However, without knowing about the Justices in Romans 2:26, the passage truly becomes impossible to understand. That's why it appeared unsolvable for 2,000 years.

Unfortunately, the inability to reconcile Paul's message caused the teaching of the original Bible to undergo a wholesale rewrite. A comparison of what Biblical scholars discuss amongst themselves versus what is included in modern versions documents this.

- Leading scholars acknowledge that the imperative verb *douleuete* has only one meaning: total and complete subservience to another (enslavement). Yet no modern Bible stays true to the one and only meaning.

- Leading scholars acknowledge that the Septuagint added "loving kindness" to the list of meanings for *dikaiosune*. Yet no modern Bible uses this information within its translation.

- Leading scholars acknowledge the extreme popularity of *Gezera Shava* during the first century. They acknowledge that "Love your neighbor as yourself" and "Love God" were prime *Gezera Shava* equivalents. Yet no modern Bible uses this information within its translation.

- The greatest Greek scholar of the Byzantine Age asserted that Romans 2:26 referred to the Torah's Code of Justice. Yet no modern Bible uses this information within its translation.

- And so on, and so on.

The manufacturers of modern Bibles wrote whatever they wanted to. Consequently, their readers remain in the dark about what the text originally taught.

- In the original text, Galatians 5:13 states that Christians are *enslaved* to loving others <u>because</u> of their obligation to the Law. This has been watered down to "serve one another in love."

- In the original text, Romans 6:18 likewise commands Christians to be enslaved to loving kindness. This has been rewritten as a command to be enslaved to moral "righteousness" instead.

- In the original text, Matthew 22:39 teaches that "Love your neighbor as yourself" is *the same* as "Love God with your whole being." Every conventional Bible has rewritten this. They all say "Love your neighbor as yourself" is *like* "Love God with your whole being."

- In the original text, Romans 2:13-26 teaches that those who keep the Justices of the Torah will be considered to have fulfilled the entire Law. This notion is entirely censored from every conventional Bible.

- In the original text, Romans 2:6-8 teaches that God will impartially judge all humanity based on their persistence in deeds of loving kindness. Modern translations have rewritten this as judgment based on ambiguous persistence in doing good.

The New Testament consistently and repeatedly taught that "Love your neighbor as yourself" is the entire Law, and those who do this inherit life in the age to come. Yet modern versions have rewritten almost every place where this message is explicitly stated in the original text. The end result? The central message of the historical Paul is not being taught in conservative churches today.

Chapter 24
Indulge Me

The original message of Paul and modern rewrites are two very different things. 1 Corinthians 6:9 is a prime example. In this verse, the historical Paul declared:

> Don't you know that the unjust will not inherit the kingdom of God? Don't fool yourselves:… not those who are *malakoi* - 1 Corinthians 6:9

Paul warned the Corinthians that 'those who are *malakoi* cannot enter the kingdom of God.' So what did it mean to be '*malakoi*'?

> The word *malakos* [singular of *malakoi*] literally means those who have become soft, **those who live for the luxuries of subtle pleasures**. It describes what we can only call **a kind of wallowing in luxury in which people have lost all resistance to pleasure**.—William Barclay (Prior Professor of Divinity and Biblical Criticism at the University of Glasgow)[188]

* * *

> Aristotle yokes *malakos* with *akolasia* and *truphē* (**licentiousness and luxury**) and defines it as "a failure to resist or be strong in the face of things that most men are able to resist" (*Nic. Eth.* 1150b1-2); **its opposite is *karteria*, fortitude** (*Nic. Eth.* 1116a14, 1150a31-b19; cf. Eur. *Suppl.* 882-85)—Victoria Wohl (Professor, Department of Classics, University of Toronto)[189]

---

188   *The Letters to the Corinthians* by William Barclay, p. 62, Westminster John Knox Press, 2002
189   *Love Among the Ruins: The Erotics of Democracy in Classical Athens* by Victoria Wohl, p. 175, Princeton University Press, 2002

The *malakoi* were self-indulgent people who were unable to resist pleasures of any kind. Professor Wohl referenced some of Aristotle's writings to document the historical meaning. Aristotle also wrote:

> **It is surprising if a man is defeated by and cannot resist pleasures** or pains which most men can hold out against, when this is not due to heredity or disease, **like the *malakia* that is hereditary with the kings of Scythians**[190]—Aristotle

Aristotle wrote that the Scythian kings were *malakoi*. How did the Scythian Kings earn that reputation? The Scythians were well known for their self-indulgent intoxication:

> Scythyians drank wine immoderately and noisily. The poet Anacreon wrote:
>
>> Come once more, let us no longer practice Scythian drinking of wine with clashing and shouting, but drink moderately with beautiful songs....[191]
>
> **The overindulgence of the Scythians** was observed by peripatetic authors, the successors of Plato's student Aristotle. Hieronymus of Rhodes in his work *On Intoxication* wrote that "'to do the Scythian' is 'to become intoxicated,'" **since the Scythians were known for their overindulgence**— Max Nelson (assistant professor of Classics at the University of Windsor)[192]

In ancient times, the *malakoi* were those who were overly self-indulgent in anything, be it food, wine, or sex. In fact, in Paul's day, even those who were self-indulgent in knowledge were called *malakoi*:

> If you spend time gaining knowledge you will be called simple-minded and *malakos*.—Dio Chrysostum (a contemporary of Paul)[193]

Paul's converts in Corinth struggled with self-indulgence in all of these things. They were self-indulgent in food,[194] sex,[195] drinking,[196]

---

190   Nic. Eth. 7.7.1150b16
191   Fragment 356(b) (Denys Page, Poetae Melici Graeci)
192   *The Barbarian's Beverage: A History of Beer in Ancient Europe* by Max Nelson, p. 42, Psychology Press, 2005
193   *The Sixty Sixth Discourse* by Dio Chrysostom, section 25.
194   1 Corinthians 6:12-13
195   1 Corinthians 6:12-13
196   1 Corinthians 5:11, 6:10

and knowledge.

How were the Corinthians self-indulgent in knowledge?

In your display of knowledge, the unsteady one has been lost, the brother or sister for whom the Messianic King died. By sinning against your brothers and sisters and assaulting their unsteady feelings, **you are sinning against the Messianic King.**[197]

The knowledgeable Corinthians knew that eating idolatrous meat was okay. So they ate it, even when it upset their weaker brothers and sisters. In this way, they were self-indulgent in knowledge. Paul's antidote to their self-indulgence in knowledge was brotherly love:

Knowledge puffs up, while love builds up.—Paul to the Corinthians[198]

Self-indulgence is the opposite of brotherly love, which is why it prevents a person from entering the kingdom of God. The Corinthians abounded in self-indulgence and were at risk of missing the kingdom because of it.

Paul's famous love chapter, often quoted at weddings, was originally written to instruct the self-indulgent Corinthians on proper Christian behavior:

Within a span of a few decades, love of neighbor, now tagged as the "Law of Christ," became—within Pauline circles and no doubt far beyond—the ultimate and only guide for a believer's conduct....

To his Corinthian converts, who were always giving him hives, Paul sent his most eloquent exposition of the life of a true believer, hoping that with such a detailed description they would finally get things straight. This is Paul's "Hymn to Love," a Himalayan peak of world literature:

And now will I show you the best Way of all.

If I speak all the tongues of men and angels, but speak without love, I am no more than a booming gong or clanging cymbal. If I can prophesy and fathom all mysteries and knowledge, and if I have so much faith that I can move mountains, but have not love, I am nothing. If I give all my possessions to the poor–and even my body that I may boast–but have not love, I gain nothing.

197   1 Corinthians 8:10-12 as translated by Dr. William Berg
198   1 Corinthians 8:1c-3 as translated by Dr. William Berg

Love is patient. Love is kind. It does not envy or boast or think highly of itself. It is not rude. It does not insist on its own way. It does not take offense, nor does it keep any record of wrongs. Love does not enjoy evil-doing but enjoys the truth. It bears all things, trusts all things, hopes all things, endures all things.

Love never ends. Prophecy will cease. Tongues will be stilled. Knowledge will fail. For we know in part and we prophesy in part, but when the Fulfillment comes, the partial will be done away with. When I was a child, I spoke as a child, I saw as a child, I thought as a child. When I became a man, I put away the things of a child. Now we see as in the distorted reflection of a glass, but then we shall see face to face. Now I know in part, then I shall know as fully as I am known.

For now, faith, hope, and love abide, these three. But the greatest of all is love.

Could the Corinthians miss the point of this large and humble essay, in which Paul, admitting what he does not know, sets out so clearly that the life of the believer is to be–at least ideally–a series of acts of generosity toward others **without regard to self-indulgence or self-seeking**? Well, the Corinthians were a difficult bunch. They required additional visits and several letters (not all of which have come down to us). Even in this letter you can read between the lines Paul's anguish at how many things they have bollixed up.—Thomas Cahill[199]

Out of all of Paul's converts, the Corinthians took the self-indulgent prize hands down. None of his other converts were even a close second in this regard. This is not surprising given that the historical city of Corinth was well known for its self-indulgent living.[200]

From both a Biblical and historical perspective, it is no wonder that Paul reminded the Corinthians that "those who are *malakoi* cannot enter the kingdom of God." In other words, it is no wonder why he reminded them:

Don't you know that the unjust will not inherit the kingdom of God? Don't fool yourselves:... not **the self-indulgent**—1 Corinthians 6:9

Once again, we come to a really big problem. For once again,

199   *Desire of the Everlasting Hills: The World Before and After Jesus* by Thomas Cahill, Random House Digital, Inc., 2001
200   *After Paul Left Corinth: The Influence of Secular Ethics and Social Change* by Bruce W. Winter, p. 88, Wm. B. Eerdmans Publishing, 2001

modern translators have taken a free hand with the Biblical text. In this case, they've written a morally repugnant sentence:

> Do you not know that the unrighteous will not inherit the kingdom of God? Do not be deceived … not **the effeminate**[201]

The NASB Bible has the audacity to claim that no effeminate man shall enter the kingdom of God. This translation is patently erroneous on three levels:

- Does Paul's letter give any indication that the Corinthians were effeminate? No. Does Paul's letter give any indication that the Corinthians were self-indulgent? Yes, very much so. Only the translation "self-indulgent" matches the contents of the letter.

- Was the Roman Empire overflowing with effeminate men? No. Was the Roman Empire overflowing with self-indulgent people? Yes, very much so. Only "self-indulgent" matches the letter's historical setting.

- Does being effeminate violate Leviticus 19:18? No, not even in the slightest. Does being self-indulgent violate Leviticus 19:18? Yes, very much so. Only "self-indulgent" matches Paul's commitment to promoting Leviticus 19:18 as the entire Law.

Modern translators ignore the issues discussed in the letter, turn a blind eye to the historical setting, and contradict Paul's (and Jesus') most fundamental teaching, all at the same time. The translators who wrote these books inserted their own prejudices while letting all the historical facts be damned.

It is alarming that the translators' own prejudices against effeminate men are now taught as God's own prejudices. The God who is discussed in modern translations is, in many ways, the opposite of the God who is discussed in the original Bible—the only Bible. The New Testament God wants his children to lovingly accept the dispositions of all manners of men (and women). Period.

---

201   1 Corinthians 6:9 NASB

Chapter 25

Red Herrings

"No effeminate man shall enter the kingdom of God" is a red herring. It distracts readers from accepting Paul's teachings that Leviticus 19:18 is the entire Law. After all, if God bans effeminate men from entering the kingdom, then "love your neighbor as yourself" isn't the only requirement. This is the danger of mistranslations.

Many Christians balk at the idea that "Love your neighbor as yourself" is the entire Law. They balk because their BINOs (Bibles in Name Only) say otherwise. But there is nothing, and I mean *nothing*, in Paul's writings that contradicts Jesus' most fundamental teaching: Fulfilling Leviticus 19:18 via the Golden Rule is the narrow road to life. In fact, Paul wrote his letters to promote Jesus' most fundamental teaching, not to destroy it.

BINOs are riddled with red herrings which prevent modern readers from accepting Leviticus 19:18 as the entire Law. They create the illusion that Paul was hyper-focused on sex as opposed to ethics. In BINOs, the Greek word *akatharsia* is rubberstamped as 'impurity,' which helps to sustain this illusion.

As you may recall, the Septuagint shaped the Jewish understanding of many Greek words. This includes *akatharsia*. Modern conventional Bibles translate this word as a reference to *sexual impurity*. However, the Septuagint had a much broader range of use for this word, including *unethical* deeds:

He is destroyed because of an *akatharsia* of the soul: an **insulting** eye, an **unjust** tongue, hands that **pour out the blood of the just**, and a heart which **devises malicious devices**, and feet that are **swift to do malice**.[202]

In the Septuagint, an *akatharsia* of the soul gives rise to a slew of unethical actions: insults, unjust speech, spilling of blood, devising malicious schemes, and reflexively doing malice. The Septuagint demonstrates that this word didn't inherently connote sexual improprieties. It could also be used to express a lack of ethics, in general.

Notice also that the Septuagint conflates *akatharsia* with using the members of the body for the unjust treatment of others:

- insulting **eye**
- unjust **tongue**
- **hands** that pour out the blood of the just
- **heart** which devises malicious devices
- **feet** that are swift to do malice

Paul's scriptures regarding the misuse of body parts share some of the same keywords ("tongue," "feet," and "blood," for example):

> There isn't anyone showing kindness, not even one.
> Their throat is an open tomb.
> They deceive with **their tongues**.
> The poison of snakes is under their lips;
> Whose mouth is filled with curses and bitterness.
> **Their feet** are eager to shed **blood**.[203]

Paul equated this specific *akatharsia* passage with his own list because *Gezera Shava* demanded it. This is why Paul mentioned *akatharsia* in his discussion on the misuse of body parts:

> Thank God you were once slaves of sin, but now have obeyed from your hearts the type of teaching that you were brought over to! Having been freed from sin, you've been enslaved to the just, fair, altruistic treatment of

202   Proverbs 6:16-17
203   Romans 3:12-15

others. (I'm speaking in human terms, taking into account the weakness of your flesh.) For **just as you once offered your bodily members for violation, as slaves to** *akatharsia* and lawlessness, so you now offer them for consecration, as slaves to the just, fair, altruistic treatment of others.

Given that Paul was steeped in the use of *Gezera Shava* and given his commitment to the Law of the Messianic King, *akatharsia* must be referring to the same unethical misuse of body parts as the Septuagint passage. "Being slaves to *akatharsia*" was equated with "using body parts for the unkind treatment of others." In other words, Paul's reference to being "slaves to *akatharsia*" in the context of Romans 6 meant "being slaves to *unethicalness*."

Thank God you were once slaves of sin, but now have obeyed from your hearts the type of teaching that you were brought over to! Having been freed from sin, you've been enslaved to the just, fair, altruistic treatment of others. (I'm speaking in human terms, taking into account the weakness of your flesh.) For **just as you once offered your bodily members for violation, as slaves to <u>unethicalness</u>** and lawlessness, so you now offer them for consecration, as slaves to the just, fair, altruistic treatment of others.

So how do the BINOs render *akatharsia* in this verse?

For just as you presented your members as slaves to **impurity**—Romans 6:19 NASB

BINOs portray Romans 6 as condemning the use of body parts for sexual impurity. Naturally, these BINOs then say that the religious remedy is to leave enslavement to sexual impurity and become enslaved to moral righteous:

For just as you presented your members as slaves to impurity and to lawlessness, resulting in further lawlessness, so now present your members as **slaves to righteousness**—Romans 6:19 NASB

What an awful change from Paul's original, very inspirational, message. Paul originally told his converts to leave enslavement to the unethical treatment of others and become slaves instead to the just, fair, altruistic treatment of others:

For just as you once offered your bodily members for violation, as **slaves to unethicalness** and lawlessness, so you now offer them for consecration, as

slaves to the just, fair, altruistic treatment of others.[204]

We must always remember that Paul's theology was founded on enslavement to loving kindness:

> **You are enslaved to one another through love** because the entire Law is fulfilled in one statement, in the precept, "Love your neighbor as yourself."[205]

BINOs use *akatharsia* to promote a mythical Paul who is hyper-focused on *purity* instead of *ethics*. They are currently getting away with this charade due to modern unawareness of the Greek Septuagint. *Akatharsia* and *akathartos* both belong to the same word group. The Septuagint used *akathartos* to mean:

- devious[206]

- devoid of altruistic deeds[207]

- unethical in business practices[208]

- proud[209]

- judging others unjustly[210]

Notice how similar this is to the list of actions engendered by an *akatharsia* of the soul.

It's very important to note that Jesus used the Greek word *akatharsia* only one time. He used it in connection with the Pharisees' hypocrisy.[211] The only passage in which Jesus used the word is devoid of sexual misconduct, yet overflowing with unethical behavior.

When a passage is dealing with sex, then "impurity" is an appropriate translation. When a passage is dealing with the unjust, unfair, unkind treatment of others, then "unethicalness" is

204   Romans 6:19
205   Galatians 5:13 as translated by Dr. William Berg
206   Compare Proverbs 3:32 LXX to Hebrew
207   Isaiah 64:5-6 LXX
208   Proverbs 20:10 LXX
209   Proverbs 16:5 LXX
210   Proverbs 17:15 LXX
211   Matthew 23:27

the appropriate translation. The English word chosen to translate *akatharsia* fully depends on the passage's topic.

The BINO word choices for *dikaiosune*, *akatharsia* and *malakos* have resulted in religious belief in a fictitious Paul. The fictitious Paul is obsessed with moral righteousness, sexual purity, and effeminacy. However, the real-world, historical Paul was laser-focused on loving kindness, ethics, and selflessness. Even his discussions on idolatry and sex were oriented around loving kindness, ethics, and selflessness.

Chapter 26

Everybody's Doing It

Paul constantly focused on the just, fair, altruistic treatment of people. In his society, the unjust, unfair, unkind treatment of others was found in abundance everywhere.   But perhaps no mistreatment of others was more visibly on display than the cruel injustice committed against young boys. During Paul's day, young boys were sodomized routinely and regularly. This sad historical fact is documented in numerous ancient sources.

For example, in an ancient theatrical play, a man is in bed with a female prostitute and says that he's looking for some "land to plow." The female prostitute responds, "If it's plowing you're after, better go to those who usually get plowed—the boys!"[212]

For men, sex with young boys was often more desirable than sex with women. This is illustrated in a play written by Quintus Novius, a near contemporary of Paul. One character nonchalantly proclaims, "*Everyone* knows that a boy is superior to a woman."[213] The character then proceeds to explain the attributes of boys that turn "everyone" on.

What age were these boys? The upper age limit was determined by body hair. The moment hair formed on the buttocks or face, the boy was too old to be desired for sex. As one first-century writer

212   Craig A. Williams. *Roman Homosexuality: Second Edition* (Kindle Locations 458-459). Kindle Edition.
213   Craig A. Williams. *Roman Homosexuality: Second Edition* (Kindle Locations 480-483). Kindle Edition.

casually declared, boys were only desired "as long as they will be able to be submissive, before their butts become hairy."[214] The moment hair grew on the buttocks or face, the boy was no longer desirable for being raped as a sex toy:

> There is no getting away from it, Roman men were attracted to young boys up to a certain age—that age may be defined as the point after puberty that the body developed hair on the buttocks and on the face.—Professor Ray Laurence (Head of the Classical and Archaeological Studies Section)[215]

What was the lower age limit? There wasn't one.

> As Niall McKeown has pointed out, **there was no lower age limit.**—Professor Ray Laurence (Head of the Classical and Archaeological Studies Section)[216]

The youngest boys were open to be raped. And raped they were... en masse. In many cases, men preferred the youngest boys. They took pleasure in the screaming and wailing produced by the destruction of their virgin innocence.[217]

It was only legal to rape slave boys. Each citizen boy wore a bracelet called a *bulla* to signify that they were off-limits for sexual rape:

> The *bulla* (the amulet of childhood) was a distinctive mark of the sexual integrity of Roman boys: it set them apart from the sexually available slave children.—Plutarch[218]

The less wealthy were forced to use their slave boys for both sex and chores. The wealthy had slave boys set aside exclusively for the purpose of sexual pleasure. The super-wealthy not only had slave boys reserved for sexual pleasure, but they also had other slaves whose sole function was to keep the boys pretty for their master. Funerary

---

214   Craig A. Williams. *Roman Homosexuality: Second Edition* (Kindle Locations 488-490). Kindle Edition.

215   *Roman Passions: A History of Pleasure in Imperial Rome* by Ray Laurence, p. 80, Continuum International Publishing Group, 2010

216   *Roman Passions: A History of Pleasure in Imperial Rome* by Ray Laurence, p. 80, Continuum International Publishing Group, 2010

217   *Roman Passions: A History of Pleasure in Imperial Rome* by Ray Laurence, p. 80, Continuum International Publishing Group, 2010

218   *Children in the Roman Empire: Outsiders Within* by Christian Laes p. 243

inscriptions mention multiple job titles designating that function.[219] For wealthy men, owning a stock of slave boy-toys was one of the most common status symbols of the day.

The sons of the family greatly desired their fathers' stock of slave boys. The satirist Martial, another near contemporary of Paul, wrote that sons so desired to rape their father's slave boys that they got busy doing so the very night of their father's death.[220] Before the corpse was even cold, the sons went straight for the slave boys.

Even the non-wealthy raped slave boys. Non-wealthy men sodomized slave boys who were prostituted by their owners. In fact, Roman calendars marked April 25th as a holiday on which men celebrated the availability of the prostituted slave boys.[221]

When it came to raping slave boys, *everybody* was doing it. I could go on and on and on about the extreme commonness of forced, nonconsensual sex with slave boys. In fact, much evidence suggests that sex with slave boys was even more popular than sex with women. It was part and parcel of everyday life. Roman citizens grew up in this environment. Paul preached Christianity in this environment. In this environment, Paul preached about the just, fair, altruistic treatment of others.

---

219   Craig A. Williams. *Roman Homosexuality: Second Edition* (Kindle Locations 665-668). Kindle Edition
220   Craig A. Williams. *Roman Homosexuality: Second Edition* (Kindle Locations 620-622). Kindle Edition.
221   Craig A. Williams. *Roman Homosexuality: Second Edition* (Kindle Locations 967-969). Kindle Edition.

Chapter 27

Prostitution

While sex with slave boys was likely the most common form of sex in the Roman Empire, sex with prostitutes ran a very close second. In Paul's day, prostitution was a legal, taxable occupation:

> Prostitution was legal (and a useful source of tax revenue)[222]—Craig S. Keener (Professor of New Testament at Asbury Theological Seminary)

*   *   *

> Prostitution was legal in Rome, and all prostitutes were required to register themselves with an aedile (urban magistrate), who would collect taxes from them. The tax, computed on a daily basis, was intended to be equal to the amount she got from her first client of the day.—Gregory S. Aldrete, Ph. D. in ancient history (Professor of History and Humanistic Studies at the University of Wisconsin)[223]

Prostitutes, in ancient Roman times, didn't just work on the streets, in brothels, at pagan temples, and in bathhouses; they were also employed to provide "room service" at inns:

> Many inns and hotels would provide prostitutes for their guests, which was regarded as a normal service. One hotel bill lists charges run up by a guest, including his room, meals, hay for his mule, and the price of a girl.—Gregory S. Aldrete, Ph. D. in ancient history (Professor of History and Humanistic Studies at the University of Wisconsin)

The charge for sex with prostitutes was conveniently itemized

---

222   *1--2 Corinthians* by Craig S. Keener, p. 59, Cambridge University Press, 2005
223   *Daily Life in the Roman City: Rome, Pompeii and Ostia* by Gregory S. Aldrete

on hotel bills.

While prostitution flourished in every city of the Roman Empire, Corinth took the cake. In Corinth, hosts of dinner parties were expected to hire travelling brothels to take care of the guests' sexual needs after they finished eating:

> For grand dinners such as the series of banquets given by the President of the Isthmian Games for the citizens of Corinth, travelling brothels could be brought in by the host to cater for guests after the dinner in the place where it was held.

> The elite who gave private banquets to which they invited clients as well as other guests provided not only for their physical hunger but also for their sexual appetites. It needs to be noted that 1 Corinthians 6:12-20 does not state that Christians actually went to brothels. They were having sexual intercourse with prostitutes in the context of the dinner.—Bruce W. Winter (Dr. Winter is a New Testament scholar and Director of the Institute for Early Christianity in the Graeco-Roman World. He is currently principal of Queensland Theological College in Australia.)[224]

∗   ∗   ∗

> There were in Roman Corinth numerous prostitutes who often served as companions of the well-to-do at meals—Ben Witherington (Bible scholar Ben Witherington is Amos Professor of New Testament for Doctoral Studies at Asbury Theological Seminary and on the doctoral faculty at St. Andrews University in Scotland.)[225]

The Corinthians grew up with prostitution all around them, so much so that prostitutes became dessert.

---

224 *After Paul Left Corinth: The Influence of Secular Ehics and Social Change* by Bruce W. Winter, p. 88, Wm. B. Eerdmans Publishing, 2001
225 *Conflict and Community in Corinth: A Socio-rhetorical Commentary on 1 and 2 Corinthians* by Ben Witherington, p. 13, Wm. B. Eerdmans Publishing, 1995

Chapter 28
Triple Prohibition

Only by understanding the first-century sexual world can we know what issues Paul was forced to confront in his ministry. Sex with prostitutes and the constant rape of slave boys competed with each other as the most common forms of sexual activity in the Roman Empire. Yet, quite interestingly, neither raping slave boys nor having sex with prostitutes was considered adultery:

> Adultery, a crime under Augustus's legislation, was defined as sex between a married woman and anyone other than her husband, so that a man who confined his extramarital activities to slaves of either sex or to prostitutes (who were usually of servile status) had nothing to fear from the law.— Philip Lyndon Reynolds (Aquinas Professor of Historical Theology at Emory's Candler School of Theology)[226]

* * *

> A married man's sexual activities with slaves, prostitutes, or other women of low status were not, in legal terms, adultery, and he could not be prosecuted. —Judith Evans Grubbs (Betty Gage Holland Professor of Roman History)[227]

Roman law forbade adultery in order to keep the family structure intact.[228] Thus, Roman men prided themselves on avoiding adultery while they were freely raping young slave boys and having sex

---

226   *To Have and to Hold: Marrying and its Documentation in Western Christendom, 400-1600* by Philip Lyndon Reynolds and John Witte, p. 50, Cambridge University Press, 2007
227   *Women and the Law in the Roman Empire: A Sourcebook on Marriage, Divorce and Widowhood* by Judith Evans Grubbs, p. 210, Psychology Press, 2002
228   *Roman Pompeii: Space and Society* by Ray Laurence, p. 61, Psychology Press, 1996. Ray Laurence is Professor in Roman History and Archaeology at the University of Kent.

with prostitutes:

> Horace reported the remarks of Cato, when he met two young men coming out of a brothel. **Cato commended their action in coming to the brothel rather than becoming involved in an adulterous affair with another man's wife** (Hor., *Sat.* 1.2.30-7, 1.2.119-34).—Professor Ray Laurence (Head of the Classical and Archaeological Studies Section at the University of Kent)[229]

* * *

> Early Roman moralists, such as Cato the Censor, Cicero, and Seneca, regarded prostitution as necessary because it prevented men from breaking up the marriages of others.—Miguel A. De La Torre (Professor of Social Ethics at the Iliff School of Theology)[230]

The men who left the brothel could have had sex with adult females, young slave boys, or both. (Brothels often included both in equal numbers.) Cato's praise of these men reflected the moral thinking of the Roman Empire. Any sex that didn't disrupt the family structure was *commendable*.

Basically, if a sexual act didn't involve a married woman, it wasn't considered adultery in the Roman Empire. This created a linguistic problem for the original Christians. If they told someone, "Don't commit adultery," then that person would say, "I don't. I only rape slave boys and have sex with prostitutes." Such a person truly considered himself to be adultery-free and highly moral in that society.

The earliest Christians needed to do more than simply say, "Don't commit adultery." They had to say: "Don't commit adultery, don't have sex with prostitutes, and don't rape young slave boys." This Triple Prohibition was one way to let converts know that marital unfaithfulness of all kinds was against the Law of the Messianic King.

One of the earliest Christian documents in existence today is the *Didache*, which was written to a first-century community to explain the teachings of the twelve apostles:

---

229   *Roman Pompeii: Space and Society* by Ray Laurence, p. 84, Taylor & Francis, 2007
230   *A Lily Among the Thorns: Imagining a New Christian Sexuality* by Miguel A. De La Torre, p. 175, John Wiley and Sons, 2007

don't murder,
don't commit adultery,
don't rape young boys,
don't have sex with prostitutes,
don't steal…[231]

The *Didache* used the Triple Prohibition to communicate the Christian concept of marital unfaithfulness.

Another first-century Christian work is the *Epistle of Barnabas*. (This work was even included with the Biblical texts for the first four hundred years of Christianity.) Barnabas 19:4 also contains the Triple Prohibition:

don't have sex with prostitutes,
don't commit adultery,
don't rape young boys[232]

The *Didache* and the *Epistle of Barnabas* document the popularity of using the Triple Prohibition to explain marital unfaithfulness to those living during Paul's day. They also further document that the two most common forms of marital unfaithfulness were raping slave boys and having intercourse with prostitutes. These were the two most common forms of marital unfaithfulness that Paul had to contend with.

---

231   Didache 2:2
232   Barnabas 19:4

Chapter 29

Decalogue Distinction

Moses' famous Ten Commandments are known as the Decalogue. The last six commandments of the Decalogue are Justices.

Last Six Decalogue Commands

5. Honor your father and mother
6. You shall not murder
7. You shall not commit adultery
8. You shall not steal
9. You shall not tell falsehoods
10. You shall not covet anything that belongs to your neighbor

The earliest Christians were intimately familiar with the Justices and their specific order in the Decalogue as well. With this in mind, notice the "murder, adultery, steal" order:

6. You shall not murder
7. You shall not commit adultery
8. You shall not steal

The *Didache*, a first-century Christian work, used the "murder, adultery, steal" order to teach about marital unfaithfulness:

don't murder,
> **don't commit adultery,**
> **don't rape young boys,**
> **don't have sex with prostitutes,**
don't steal…[233]

---

233   Didache 2:2

This first-century Christian text used the Decalogue's order to communicate its condemnation of the three common ways of being unfaithful: having sex with a married woman, raping a slave boy, and having intercourse with a prostitute.

Decalogue	Didache
Do not murder	Do not murder
Do not commit adultery	**Do not have sex with married women** **Do not rape young boys** **Do not have sex with prostitutes**
Do not steal	Do not steal

This technique of using the Decalogue's order to explain adultery was very popular among the earliest Christians. Take Clement of Alexandria, a second-century Church Father, as another example:

You shall not murder
You shall not commit adultery
You shall not rape young boys
You shall not steal
You shall not tell falsehoods about your neighbor[234]

Notice how Clement's work further documents the extreme popularity of raping slave boys as an extra-marital pastime.

Decalogue	Clement of Alexandria
Do not murder	Do not murder
Do not commit adultery	**Do not have sex with married women** **Do not rape young boys**
Do not steal	Do not steal
Do not tell falsehoods	Do not tell falsehoods against your neighbor

In early Christian sin lists, the prohibitions relative to the

234   *Exhortation to the Greeks*, Clement of Alexandria

seventh commandment refer to either:

- Adultery (sex with a married woman)

- Raping slave boys

- Sex with prostitutes

It is extremely important to recognize how common it was for the earliest Christians to list 'raping young boys' relative to the seventh commandment. This is a critical piece of historical information, for it allows us to understand the precise meaning of the ancient Greek word *arsenokoitai*. Below is a first-century Christian sin list which contains this crucial word:

> those who murder their fathers and mothers,
> murderers,
>> those who have sex with married women,[235]
>> the *arsenokoitai*,
> men-stealers,
> liars,
> perjurers

This ancient Christian sin list is structured around the Decalogue.

Decalogue	*Ancient Christian Sin List*
Honor your father and mother	Murderers of fathers and mothers
Do not murder	Murderers
Do not commit adultery	Those who have sex with married women **The *arsenokoitai***
Do not steal	Stealers of men
Do not tell falsehoods about your neighbor	Liars and perjurers

As previously documented, early Christian sin lists consistently listed *the rape of slave boys* relative to the seventh commandment—

235   See chapter 34, "Christian Catchphrase," and chapter 35, "Lady Stealers" for documentation of this translation

which was only natural, given that raping slave boys was the most common form of marital unfaithfulness at that time. Therefore, in the above sin list, *arsenokoitai* must have meant "rape of slave boys."

Where is this sin list found? It is found in the Bible. It is found in 1 Timothy.

Modern Biblical scholars recognize that the 1 Timothy sin list corresponds to the Decalogue:

> The last half of the vice list in 1 Tim 1:9-10, at least, corresponds to the order of the Decalogue:
>
> Fifth commandment (honor one's parents) = "murderers of fathers and mothers"
> Sixth commandment (do not murder) = "murderers"
> Seventh commandment (do not commit adultery) = *pornoi, arsenokoitai*
> Eighth commandment (do not steal) = *andrapodistai* (men-stealers)
> Ninth commandment (do not bear false witness) = "liars, perjurers"
> – Dan Otto Via (Professor Emeritus of New Testament at Duke University Divinity School)[236]

Perhaps the more unusual word in the sin list is "men-stealers." Dr. Via explains that early Judeo-Christian sin lists commonly listed "stealers of men" (*andrapodistai*) relative to the eighth commandment. He cites Pseudo-Phocylides, Philo, the *Didache*, and *Barnabas* as examples:

> *Andrapodistai* finds its place under the distinct heading of the eighth commandment against stealing (Pseudo-Phocylides 3-8; Philo, *Special Laws* 3.1-82; 4.13-19; *Didache* 2:2-3; *Barnabas* 19:4).—Dan Otto Via (Professor Emeritus of New Testament at Duke University Divinity School)[237]

1 Timothy follows the standard Judeo-Christian sin list structure. Therefore, we know precisely what its author wrote.

---

236   *Homosexuality and the Bible: Two Views* by Dan Otto Via, Robert A. J. Gagnon p.87 Fortress Press, 2003
237   *Homosexuality and the Bible: Two Views* by Dan Otto Via, Robert A. J. Gagnon p.87 Fortress Press, 2003

Decalogue	1 Timothy Sin List
Honor your father and mother	Murderers of fathers and mothers
Do not murder	Murderers
Do not commit adultery	Those who have sex with married women **Those who rape slave boys**
Do not steal	Stealers of men
Do not tell falsehoods about your neighbor	Liars and perjurers

It cannot be emphasized enough that *raping slave boys* was associated with the seventh commandment.

- The *Didache* documents "not raping young boys" as an extension of the seventh commandment.

- *The Epistle of Barnabas* documents "not raping young boys" as an extension of the seventh commandment.

- Clement of Alexandria documents "not raping young boys" as an extension of the seventh commandment.

The *arsenokoitai*, then, were the rapists of young slave boys. The *Epistle of Barnabas*, the *Didache*, and Clement of Alexandria, combined with 1 Timothy, document this. The historical record regarding the extreme commonness of raping slave boys also makes the issue abundantly clear.

The historical record shows that 1 Timothy used the Decalogue to communicate its condemnation of those who rape young slave boys:

> law does not apply to the altruistic person, but to ... **those who rape young slave boys**...

The author of 1 Timothy condemned the sodomizing of young boys by otherwise heterosexual men. He, like other Christian authors, used the Decalogue to condemn this common, cruel injustice.

Sadly, modern conventional Bibles completely disregard 1 Timothy's Decalogue framework:

law is not made for a righteous person, but for ... homosexuals

Modern conventional Bibles claim that no homosexual shall enter the kingdom of God. From a historical perspective, virtually every heterosexual Roman male was both a womanizer and a rapist of young boys. Given that 1 Timothy used *arsenokoitai* relative to the seventh commandment, we know that the passage was actually condemning these heterosexual rapists of slave boys, not homosexuals.

Once again, we find that modern books masquerading as Bibles contain a prejudicial statement which is patently erroneous on three levels:

- Does any Koine Christian sin list mention *homosexuality* relative to the seventh commandment? No, none do. Do Koine Christian sin lists mention *raping young boys* relative to the seventh commandment? Yes, very much so. Therefore, only "rapists of young boys" matches 1 Timothy's use of the Decalogue in this passage.

- Historically speaking, were the rapists of slave boys heterosexual or homosexual? When it came to adult sex, they slept with women, not men. It was the macho, heterosexual men who were raping slave boys.[238] "Homosexuals" is historically incorrect. Therefore, only "rapists of young boys" matches the real-world situation being addressed in 1 Timothy.

- Do consenting same-sex relationships violate Leviticus 19:18? No, not even in the slightest. Does the rape of young boys violate Leviticus 19:18? Yes, very much so. Only "rapists of young boys" matches Paul's commitment to promoting Leviticus 19:18 as the entire Law.

---

238   Craig A. Williams. *Roman Homosexuality: Second Edition* (Kindle Locations 488-490). Kindle Edition. Note that the first-century writer mentioned that boys are only desired "until their butts become hairy." Adult males were a turnoff. Ergo, the men in question desired females when it came to their adult sex life. They were heterosexual.

Conventional translations ignore the context of the letter (the Decalogue), turn a blind eye to the historical setting, and contradict Paul's (and Jesus') most fundamental teaching, all at the same time. The translators who wrote these books were so desperate to insert their own prejudices that, once again, they let all the historical facts be damned.

Modern translators destroy Paul's Gospel. Paul wrote his letters to teach that only the commandments based on "Love your neighbor as yourself" are the Law. He went to great pains to make sure that his discussions on sex couldn't be misconstrued as opposing this. Yet conventional Bibles misconstrue his writings anyway.

Chapter 30

Lay of the Land

Conventional translators not only contradicted 1 Timothy's immediate context (the Decalogue), but they also contradicted the general context as well. Quite ironically, the 1 Timothy passage was written to teach that love is the point of the entire Law:

> **The ultimate goal of our instruction is love** from a pure heart, a good conscience, and sincere faith; **some have missed that point**, and have been diverted into pointless ruminations, **meaning to be teachers of the law, but not understanding either what they are saying or what they are making their assertions about …**

> However, we know that the law is a fine thing if you use it lawfully, with the knowledge that law does not apply to those who treat others justly, but only to … those who kill their parents and to murderers and those who have sex with married women and boy-rapers (*arsenokoitai*) and men stealers and liars and perjurers[239]

Conventional translations replace 'boy-rapers' with 'homosexuals.' Ironically, in a passage designed to teach that love is the entire Law, the authors of modern Bibles wrote a list that teaches that love is not the entire Law. The irony would be comical if the modern consequences weren't so severe.

The author of this passage railed against Christians who wanted to teach others, but didn't understand that the whole point of the Law was love. Therefore, he made a list of unloving people who need the

---

239   1 Timothy 1:5-10

Law.   Were the rapists of slave boys inherently unloving?   Yes, very much so.   Are homosexuals inherently unloving?   No, of course not. The Decalogue framework already informs us that the rapists of slave boys were the ones being condemned.   The topic of *unloving people* independently informs us of the very same thing.

It's hard to know why the authors of modern Bibles wrote what they did.   They contradict the Decalogue framework of the immediate context.   They also oppose the general context (a discussion on why love is the entirety of the Law).   Conventional translations vehemently oppose the passage's original teaching.   As a result, they convince millions to fiercely oppose it too.

Chapter 31

The Bible Tells Me So

Christian conservatives claim to be the ones upholding the Bible. They accuse liberals of rejecting the message of the Biblical text. But is this true?

Let's take a second look at the Christian conservative's perspective on homosexuality:

St. Paul makes an explicit statement condemning homosexual practice in his letter to the Romans:

God gave them over in the sinful desires of their hearts to sexual impurity for the degrading of their bodies with one another. They exchanged the truth of God for a lie, and worshiped and served created things rather than the Creator-who is forever praised. Amen. Because of this, God gave them over to shameful lusts. **Even their women exchanged natural relations for unnatural ones. In the same way the men also abandoned natural relations with women and were inflamed with lust for one another. Men committed indecent acts with other men, and received in themselves the due penalty for their perversion.** ¯*Romans 1:24-27*

There are lists of disobedient types of people, including homosexuals, that are condemned in St. Paul's other letters, specifically I Corinthians and I Timothy:

Do you not know that the unrighteous will not inherit the kingdom of God? Do not be deceived; neither fornicators, nor idolaters, nor adulterers, **nor effeminate, nor homosexuals** (also trans.:

sexual perverts), nor thieves, nor {the} covetous, nor drunkards, nor revilers, nor swindlers, will inherit the kingdom of God.—*1 Corinthians 6:9-10*

The law is not laid down for the just but for the lawless and disobedient, for the ungodly and sinners, for the unholy and profane, for murderers of fathers and murderers of mothers, for manslayers, immoral persons, sodomites [**homosexuals**], kidnapers, liars, perjurers, and whatever else is contrary to sound doctrine.—*1 Timothy 1:9-10*

There is no scriptural reference that can be found to support the purported morality of homosexuality. So, **the testimony of Scripture is irrefutable in its prohibition of homosexuality and emphatic in its condemnation of those who practice it. There is no honest way around this issue, as inconvenient as it may be to people of the present day who revel in the dark pleasures of homosexual intercourse, and enable others to do the same.**[240]—Reverend Wheeler (pastor of Holy Cross Church)

When it comes to homosexuality, the conservative perspective rests on three Pauline passages:

1. 1 Timothy 1:9-10

2. 1 Corinthians 6:9-10

3. Romans 1:24-27

But is there any validity to the claim that these scriptures are "irrefutable in their prohibition of homosexuality and emphatic in their condemnation of those who practice it"? The conservative NASB Bible certainly claims that 1 Timothy 1:9-10 condemns homosexuality:

realizing the fact that **law is not made for a righteous person, but for those who are** lawless and rebellious, for the ungodly and sinners, for the unholy and profane, for those who murder their fathers or mothers, for murderers and immoral men and **homosexuals** and kidnappers and liars and perjurers, and whatever else is contrary to sound teaching[241]

However, as we've already noted, the author of 1 Timothy condemned the boy-raping *arsenokoitai*, not homosexuals. He

---

240   "The Abomination of Homosexuality in the Episcopal Church" by Fr. Lawrence B. "Chip" Wheeler, January 9, 2010
241   1 Timothy 1:9–10 NASB

presented his condemnation in a sin list based on the Decalogue, where *arsenokoitai* is mentioned relative to the seventh commandment. The historical record shows that the rape of slave boys was the extension of the seventh commandment in early Christian sin lists. Thus, the historical record shows the author of 1 Timothy used the Decalogue framework to condemn the rape of young boys, not to condemn homosexual relationships.

History also shows us that those who raped young boys commonly had sex with adult women. They were repulsed by the idea of having sex with adult males. When it came to the adult part of their sex life, they were heterosexual.[242] Biblically and historically speaking, homosexuals aren't even mentioned in the original 1 Timothy passage. The original passage condemned the heterosexual rapists of young boys. It is rather unfortunate that modern conventional translators have changed it.

It bears repeating that 1 Timothy 1:9-10 was written to condemn those who want to teach about the Bible "even though they do not understand either what they are saying or the matters about which they make confident assertions."

> **But the goal of our instruction is love** from a pure heart and a good conscience and a sincere faith. **For some men, straying from these things, have turned aside to fruitless discussion, wanting to be teachers of the Law, even though they do not understand either what they are saying or the matters about which they make confident assertions.** But we know that the Law is good, if one uses it lawfully[243]

The passage basically says that Christians who don't know that love is the entirety of the Law don't know what they are talking about. The passage chastises those who want to teach others, yet do not understand that the just and altruistic treatment of others is the entire point.[244]   Ironically, the passage is condemning Reverend Wheeler

---

242   Craig A. Williams. *Roman Homosexuality: Second Edition* (Kindle Locations 488-490). Kindle Edition. Note that the first-century writer mentioned that boys are only desired "until their butts become hairy." Adult males were a turnoff. Ergo, the men in question desired females when it came to their adult sex life. They were heterosexual.

243   1 Timothy 1:5–8 NASB

244   1 Timothy 1:9 uses the term *dikaioi* which commonly referred to those who treat others justly and altruistically; most especially within the context of a passage on love. Jesus used the term *dikaioi* to refer to those who feed the hungry, clothe the naked, and shelter the homeless in Matthew 25:31-46. *Dikaioi*

and others who quote 1 Timothy to boldly claim that loving others isn't the entire Christian obligation. It is to these folks, who condemn homosexuality, that 1 Timothy says, "You do not understand what you are saying."

What about 1 Corinthians 6:9-10? Does Paul contradict 1 Timothy's statement that love is the entire point of the Law? Does Paul contradict his own teaching that "love your neighbor as yourself" is the entire Law? Does Paul contradict his own teaching that bearing the burdens of others fulfills the Law of the Messianic King? The NASB Bible claims that he does:

> Or do you not know that the unrighteous will not inherit the kingdom of God? Do not be deceived; neither … **effeminate**, nor **homosexuals**… will inherit the kingdom of God.[245]

The Greek word that is translated as "homosexuals" was *arsenokoitai*. As 1 Timothy made abundantly clear, this word referred to the rapists of slave boys, not those who are engaged in adult homosexual relationships.

The Greek word translated as 'effeminate' was *malakoi*. As we documented earlier, Paul used this word to condemn the self-indulgent Corinthians, not the effeminate ones.

Paul originally wrote 1 Corinthians 6:9-10 to condemn unloving people, just as the original 1 Timothy sin list did. Unfortunately, Paul's lists of unloving people have been discarded and replaced with prejudicial, bigoted lists instead. Many Christians today quote words written by intolerant men as if they were the words of God himself. The faster humanity can move beyond this regrettable situation, the better. Discrimination has no place in the Christian Faith.

Finally, does Romans "make an explicit statement condemning homosexual practice," as Reverend Wheeler claims?

---

belongs to the same word group as *dikaiosune* and therefore was related to loving kindness in the early Judeo-Christian tradition. See chapter 10, "Jobless," for more information on *dikaioi*.

245   1 Corinthians 6:9–10 NASB

- First, Romans made an explicit statement regarding goddess cults, combined with idolatry, combined with homosexuality, combined with orgies. It doesn't contain an explicit statement about homosexuality itself, let alone homosexual relationships.

- Second, Paul purposefully separated the cultic idolatrous homosexual orgies from sins worthy of spiritual death. (This is how we know that the type of idolatrous homosexual orgy activities that he wrote about didn't involve adultery. This is how we know that the activities must have been committed by single adults.)

- Third, the historical record reveals that there were multiple instances of idolatrous pre-marital homosexual orgies in ancient goddess religions matching Paul's description.

Romans doesn't contain an explicit statement about homosexual relationships, as Reverend Wheeler confidently asserts. Rather, it contains an explicit statement about orgiastic cults, plus idolatry, plus homosexuality. This behavioral mix, reprehensible as it was to Paul, did not amount to a sin worthy of spiritual death. So what about homosexuality, *minus* cults, *minus* idolatry, *minus* orgies?

Paul's letter to the Romans specified that the idolatrous homosexual orgy practices caused the participants to "receive within themselves" the necessary penalty. Theologians debate the precise nature of the physical penalty. But whatever the physical penalty was for the cultic, idolatrous, homosexual orgies, will a monogamous gay couple receive a physical penalty in themselves for their marriage? Of course not. The consequence of cultic, idolatrous, homosexual orgy practices doesn't apply to gay marriage. In other words, *the passage doesn't apply to gay marriage.* Period.

Those who quote Romans against gay marriage are contradicting the historical setting, turning a blind eye to Paul's reference to idolatry, and overlooking the fact that Paul separated the idolatrous, homosexual orgies from sins worthy of spiritual death. Neither the historical setting nor the passage's idolatrous context nor the deliberate separation allow for an anti-gay marriage interpretation. Anti-gay marriage theology exists *despite* Romans, not in light of it.

There isn't a single passage from Paul that can validly be used to condemn the ordination of gay clergy or the institution of gay marriage. In fact, the Paul who wrote that loving others fulfills the entire Law is the last person that modern conservatives should try to appeal to. In their obsession to condemn homosexuals, they pervert Paul's most fundamental teaching. We must help these conservatives see the errors of their ways in order to help them avoid the just condemnation for their anti-Paul, anti-Biblical teachings.

It must also be pointed out that some conservatives appeal to the Old Testament book of Leviticus, in addition to Paul, in order to bolster their condemnation of homosexuals:

> Centuries later, the law was given to Moses—not just the Ten Commandments, but also all of the statutes of the Torah: moral and ethical laws, as well as ritual and dietary regulations. This is what Leviticus says about homosexual practice:
>
>> You shall not lie with a male as one lies with a female (also trans.: practice homosexuality); it is an abomination. (also trans.: detestable sin).—Leviticus 18:22
>>
>> If a man lies with a man as one lies with a woman, both of them have done what is detestable (an abomination). They must be put to death; their blood will be on their own heads.—Leviticus 20:13.[246]
>
> —Reverend Wheeler (pastor of Holy Cross Church)

Reverend Wheeler asserts that Moses' entire moral code remains in force today, including the Leviticus prohibition of homosexuality. Why does he believe this? Reverend Wheeler explains:

> **The moral laws of Moses contained in the Hebrew Scriptures of the Old Testament still stand, because our Lord himself said that they still stand.** By saying that, Jesus passed on the moral law of Moses as part of the deposit of faith which he commanded to be continued. Witness the words of Jesus in the Sermon on the Mount in St. Matthew's Gospel, chapter five:

246   "The Abomination of Homosexuality in the Episcopal Church" by Fr. Lawrence B. "Chip" Wheeler, January 9, 2010

> **Do not think that I came to abolish the Law or the Prophets**; I did not come to abolish but to fulfill. For truly I say to you, until heaven and earth pass away, not the smallest letter or stroke shall pass from the Law until all is accomplished. **Whoever then annuls one of the least of these commandments, and teaches others {to do} the same, shall be called least in the kingdom of heaven**; but whoever keeps and teaches {them,} he shall be called great in the kingdom of heaven.—Matthew 5:17-19

> Radical leaders of society or the Church may consider moral values to be changeable with the times. However, that notion is not true. The basic moral values that were established by God from the beginning are reflected in the unwritten natural law, and specifically promulgated in the written law of Moses. This law was not superceded [*sic*] by the new covenant established through Jesus Christ.—Reverend Wheeler (pastor of Holy Cross Church)[247]

It is interesting that Reverend Wheeler quotes Matthew 5:17-19 in isolation. Atheist organizations, such as EvilBible.com, quote this passage in isolation too.[248] They, however, use it to claim that Jesus taught that the *entire* Law was preserved.[249]

So what about Paul? Did Paul believe that Jesus preserved the entire Law (as EvilBible.com says) or only the moral code (as Reverend Wheeler says)? Or did he believe Jesus taught something entirely different?

---

247 "The Abomination of Homosexuality in the Episcopal Church" by Fr. Lawrence B. "Chip" Wheeler, January 9, 2010
248 http://www.evilbible.com/do_not_ignore_ot.htm, September 1, 2011
249 http://www.evilbible.com/do_not_ignore_ot.htm, September 1, 2011

Chapter 32

The Leviticus List

Jesus wasn't the only one who talked about preserving the Law. Paul did too:

> Are we abolishing the law through the Faith? In no way! Rather we are establishing it.[250]

So how can we possibly reconcile this with Paul's other teachings? Actually, there's nothing to even reconcile. All we have to do is to read what Paul wrote in the context of the rest of the letter:

> Are we abolishing the law through the Faith? In no way! Rather we are establishing it…. because he who loves others has fulfilled the law, because "don't commit adultery," "don't murder," "don't steal," "don't covet," and any other commandment are all summed up in this precept: "Love your neighbor as yourself."[251]

To understand Paul's teaching on the Law, we must take all of his teachings together. When we do, we find that his point is really, really simple. In fact, it's so simple that a child can understand it. It all boils down to a single idea:

The Christian Faith preserves the Law because only the commandments based on Leviticus 19:18 are the Law.

There you have it! No mystery there. No contradiction. Simply take Paul's statements together, and what he wrote actually becomes

---

250   Romans 3:31
251   Romans 3:31, 13:8-9

very clear.

But where did Paul get this idea in the first place? Ironically, he got it from the very same place that Reverend Wheeler and EvilBible.com quoted from. He got the idea from Jesus' Sermon on the Mount.

Reverend Wheeler and EvilBible.com both quote the beginning of Jesus' famous sermon, and they both leave out the ending punch line:

> I have not come to abolish the Law and the Prophets... In everything, therefore, treat others the same way you want to be treated: for this is the Law and the Prophets.—Jesus[252]

Reverend Wheeler and EvilBible.com both quote the setup while leaving out the surprising twist.

As you may recall, the Golden Rule was the official Jewish method for fulfilling Leviticus 19:18.[253] In other words, Jesus delivered the Sermon on the Mount in order to teach:

I haven't come to abolish the Law because only the commandments based on Leviticus 19:18 are the Law.

Now compare this to Paul's letter to the Romans:

The Christian Faith doesn't abolish the Law, because only the commandments based on Leviticus 19:18 are the Law.

Jesus said it. Paul believed it. And that settled it for Paul.

Jesus' Sermon on the Mount didn't endorse the entirety of the Mosaic moral code. On the contrary, it endorsed all the commandments based on Leviticus 19:18.[254] In other words, it preserved all the Justices of the Torah and only the Justices of the Torah. Hence, Paul wrote his letters to teach his converts about the Justices, so that they too could

---

252   Matthew 5:17, 7:12 (both verses are part of the same sermon—the Sermon on the Mount)
253   As documented in chapter 8, "Detour"
254   Jesus repeatedly taught that *only* the commandments based on "Love your neighbor as yourself" are the Law. In other words, he repeatedly affirmed that the entire Mosaic moral code is *not* preserved. See Matthew 19:16-19 for another example.

follow Jesus.

Isolating the beginning of the sermon, while knowing the ending twist, is disingenuous at best. Using the isolated, out-of-context, quote to claim the preservation of Moses' entire moral code is untenable. It also demonstrates an unawareness of the historical division of Jewish law. The most fundamental division of Jewish law was the division into Justices and Jobs. Philo, a contemporary of Paul, does a superb job of explaining the legal division that existed during their day:

> And there are, as we may say, two most especially important heads of all the innumerable particular lessons and doctrines; the regulating of one's conduct towards God by the rules of piety and holiness, and of one's conduct towards men by the rules of humanity and justice; each of which is subdivided into a great number of subordinate ideas, all praiseworthy.— Philo Judaeus (first-century Jewish author)[255]

Purity issues (both dietary and sexual) were Jobs (commandments between man and God). The humanitarian, ethical rules (commandments based on Leviticus 19:18) were Justices. Jesus' Sermon on the Mount was directed at the division of the Law that existed during his day. He delivered the sermon to teach that he hadn't come to abolish the Law, because only the Justices are the Law. Paul's letters dutifully reflect this.

Paul didn't condemn the idolatrous homosexual orgy practices as sins worthy of spiritual death because that's a purity issue. It's a violation of the Jobs. If he labeled it as a sin worthy of spiritual death, then he'd be contradicting himself. He'd be contradicting his own statement that only the commandments based on Leviticus 19:18 are the Law. He'd be contradicting Jesus, too.

Paul's letters are virtually impossible to understand without an awareness of the Justices and the Jobs. Two thousand years of failing to reconcile Romans 1–3 is sufficient historical evidence of this. Modern theologians, like Reverend Wheeler, continue to misconstrue Paul's writings because of their own unawareness of the Justices and the Jobs. Yet, ironically, the moment the Justices and the Jobs are understood,

---

255   The Special Laws 2.63 by Philo Judaeus

Paul's letters immediately become the easiest books to understand. It turns out that Paul, the learned ex-Pharisee, crafted all his letters around the traditional division of Jewish law that existed during his day—the Justices and the Jobs.

Chapter 33

Legal Labyrinth

Paul applied his understanding of the Justices and the Jobs to absolutely everything, including heterosexuality. This is readily demonstrated by contrasting his legal treatment of adultery with his treatment of pre-marital sex with prostitutes.

In Paul's theology, "don't commit adultery" was part of Christian Law:

> he who loves others has fulfilled the Law because **"don't commit adultery,"** "don't murder," "don't steal," "don't covet," and if there is any other commandment it is summed up in these words: "You shall love your neighbor as yourself."—Paul[256]

Paul believed that only the doers of the Law would be vindicated before God. And adultery was one of the acts that a person could commit to break the Law:

> **The doers of the law are those who will be vindicated....**
>
> You're preaching not to steal, and you're stealing! **You're saying not to commit adultery, and you're committing adultery!** Idols disgust you, but you plunder their temples! You speak loudly of law, but **you bring dishonor on God by breaking the law!** "Thanks to you, the name of God is being profaned among the heathen," just as it is written.[257]

---

256   Romans 13:8-9
257   Romans 2:13, 21-24. Note: Most translations have question marks for Romans 2:21-23. However, the lack of interrogative particles in the Greek indicates a series of exclamations rather than questions.

In Paul's theology, committing adultery was one of his examples of breaking the Law. In other words, adultery was *unlawful*.

Now let's compare this to Paul's legal treatment of pre-marital sex with prostitutes.[258] When addressing this issue, he wrote:

> **Everything is lawful to me**, but not everything is good for me. **Everything is lawful to me**, but I am not one who will be dominated by anyone. Food is there for the stomach, yes, and the stomach is there for food, and God will put an end to both of them. **Your whole body, however, is there not for sex with prostitutes**[259]

When writing about pre-marital sex with prostitutes, Paul wrote that everything is lawful. Where did this phrase "everything is lawful" come from?

We already know that Paul told the Romans that adultery was unlawful. In fact, he told them that adultery was so unlawful that those who do it cannot be vindicated before God. So why didn't he use the same language with the Corinthians when discussing pre-marital sex with prostitutes? Why didn't he simply tell them that they were violating the Law just like he said to the Romans? He couldn't. So he didn't. Adultery is a violation of the Justices and pre-marital sex with prostitutes isn't. In the context of pre-marital sex with prostitutes, everything really is lawful.

I have looked into more than a dozen commentaries on Paul's statement, "everything is lawful to me." None of their analyses factor in his statement that adultery is unlawful. They are overlooking the most critical piece of information necessary for understanding Paul's point. For when these two concepts are brought together, they converge on revealing the theological core of the historical Paul.

Allow me to demonstrate. There are three basic Christian camps:

---

258   Paul shows that he's addressing single people in 1 Corinthians 7:2, "But because of prostitutions, each man is to have his own wife, and each woman is to have her own husband." Many Bibles wrongly say, "But because of immoralities..." This is yet another red herring.
259   1 Corinthians 6:12-13 as translated by Dr. William Berg

- Those who believe that Christians are not under any law whatsoever

- Those who believe that Christians are bound to Moses' entire moral code

- Those who believe that the Golden Rule is the entire Law

Obviously, only one of these camps shares the same theology as Paul. So how can we determine which one? The convergence of the following two concepts tells us everything we need to know:

- Adultery is unlawful.

- In the context of pre-marital sex, everything is lawful.

The 'no law' camp opposes 'adultery is unlawful.'

The 'Mosaic moral code' camp opposes 'everything is lawful.'

Only the 'Golden Rule' camp embraces both notions. Because of the Golden Rule, adultery is unlawful. Because of the Golden Rule, within the context of pre-marital sex, everything really is lawful.

Conservative theologians populate the first two camps. Liberals take up residence in the 'Golden Rule' camp. Only the 'Golden Rule' camp advocates the historical Paul's teachings *as a whole*. Only the 'Golden Rule' camp embraces everything Paul wrote.

We can also think of this in terms of the Justices and the Jobs. Adultery violates the Justices. Therefore, it is unlawful. Pre-marital sex with prostitutes doesn't violate the Justices. Therefore, everything within this context is lawful (albeit not necessarily beneficial). It's really no more complicated than that. As we have seen over and over again, Paul's writings are simple and straightforward the moment a person understands the Justices and the Jobs.

We find, within Paul's legal labyrinth, a very simple principle. Any sexual act that violates the Justices is unlawful; whether it is an act involving a member of the opposite sex (e.g. adultery) or same sex (e.g. raping boys). Any sexual act that doesn't violate the Justices is lawful;

whether it is an act involving a member of the opposite sex (e.g. pre-marital sex with prostitutes) or same sex (e.g. cultic idolatrous same-sex orgy fests). In other words, Paul judged the legality of sexual acts using the same standard that he applied to everything else. He was perfectly consistent. It is time for Christianity to finally understand the man.

Chapter 34
Christian Catchphrase

Preventing marital infidelity was one of Paul's greatest concerns. Adultery was considered one of the gravest sins in the culture in which he was reared — or more specifically, adultery on the part of a married woman was considered one of the gravest sins:

> In Jewish as in most other societies, the adultery of the husband against the wife was not an issue (Num 5:11-31). Adultery signified only the marital unfaithfulness of the wife to the husband. This is because the sexuality of the wife was said to belong to the husband who, besides, could marry more than one wife (see Deut 22:13-27...)—Fernando F. Segovia (Oberlin Graduate Professor of New Testament and Early Christianity at Vanderbuilt University)[260]

* * *

> Traditional Jewish law defines adultery as a sexual encounter between a married woman and a man not her husband. An affair between a married man and a single woman is not considered adultery.—Rabbi Michael Gold[261]

In Judaism, a wife's adultery was considered far more offensive than that of a husband.

A cheating wife was considered to be a "whore." Therefore, the Greek word for "prostitute" became an epithet for married women

---

260   *Reading from this Place: Social Location and Biblical Interpretation in Global Perspective* by Fernando F. Segovia, Mary Ann Tolbert, p. 62, Fortress Press, 1995
261   *Does God Belong in the Bedroom?* by Rabbi Michael Gold, p. 49, Jewish Publication Society, 1992

who committed adultery: [262]

> Because of its association with "playing the prostitute," *porneia* sometimes represents marital infidelity in the Septuagint—Craig S. Keener (Professor of New Testament at Asbury Theological Seminary)[263]

* * *

> *Porneia* was typically used when referring to **female adultery.**—Dr. Mark E. Moore (professor of New Testament at Ozark Christian College)[264]

The Decalogue considered married women to be the property of their husbands. Any man who committed *porneia*—any man who had sex with a married woman—was therefore trespassing against the husband:

> the Decalogue included a wife as a man's possession. (Ex. 20:14, Dt. 5:21). Like a married wife, a betrothed girl was punishable for adultery, as was any man having intercourse with her. Throughout the ancient Near East, whether a female was betrothed or married, seduction or rape was **a trespass against her husband.**—Étan Levine (emeritus professor at the University of Haifa specializing in Jewish Bible commentary and Rabbinics)[265]

Any man who had sexual intercourse with either a betrothed or married woman was trespassing against the husband. In other words, sexual intercourse with another man's woman (*porneia*) was considered *cheating a brother*:

> Here is the will of God, here is what makes you holy: **you stay away from porneia**, each one of you knowing how to keep your own body in a state of holiness and honor, and not in a state of passion like the Gentiles who don't know God—which means not trying to get around and **cheat your brother in the process**, because when it comes to all such things the Master is the avenger, just as we have told you and testified to before.—Paul[266]

Paul, like other first-century Jews, considered *porneia* to constitute cheating a brother. Notice that the passage indisputably shows that he used *porneia* to refer to sexual intercourse with another

262   The Greek word for "prostitute" was *pornē* from which the Greeks derived *porneia* (prostitution).
263   *A Commentary on the Gospel of Matthew* by Craig S. Keener, p. 467, Wm. B. Eerdmans Publishing, 2005
264   *The Chronological Life of Christ* by Mark E. Moore, p. 177, College Press, 2007
265   *Marital Relations in Ancient Judaism* by Étan Levine, p. 178, Otto Harrassowitz Verlag, 2009
266   1 Thessalonians 4:3-6 as translated by Dr. William Berg

man's woman. He simply used the extended Judeo-Christian meaning of the word:

> Here is the will of God, here is what makes you holy: **you stay away from sex with another man's wife**, each one of you knowing how to keep your own body in a state of holiness and honor, and not in a state of passion like the Gentiles who don't know God—which means not trying to get around and **cheat your brother in the process**, because when it comes to all such things the Master is the avenger, just as we have told you and testified to before.—Paul[267]

How do modern conventional Bibles translate this passage? They disregard the context and insert their own doctrine:

> For this is the will of God, your sanctification; that is, that you abstain from **sexual immorality**; that each of you know how to possess his own vessel in sanctification and honor, not in lustful passion, like the Gentiles who do not know God; and that no man transgress and defraud his brother in the matter[268]

While it is very beneficial to abstain from sexual immorality, this passage simply has nothing to do with this broad concept. The passage specifically addresses sexual intercourse with another man's woman. Mistranslating it as "sexual immorality" severely distorts Paul's message. It's another red herring. It distracts the reader from recognizing Paul's steadfast commitment to promoting Leviticus 19:18 as the entire Law.

Quite interestingly, Jesus himself also used *porneia* in reference to sexual intercourse with another man's woman:

> but I say to you that everyone who divorces his wife, except for the reason of *porneia*, makes her commit adultery; and whoever marries a divorced woman commits adultery.—Jesus[269]

Jesus, like Paul, used the extended Judeo-Christian meaning of *porneia*.

Very often, when you see "sexual immorality" in modern Bibles, the author is specifically referring to "sex with another man's

267   1 Thessalonians 4:3-6 as translated by Dr. William Berg
268   1 Thessalonians 4:3-6 NASB
269   Matthew 5:32

woman." The rubberstamped use of "sexual immorality" is yet another red herring. It prevents the reader from seeing Paul's careful separation of sexual practices which violate the Justices from those that don't. "Sex with another man's wife" violates the Justices—it "cheats a brother in the process." Thus, not having sex with another man's wife is *a commandment of Jesus*:

> For **you know the commandments we gave you via the Master Jesus.** Here is the will of God, here is what makes you holy: you **stay away from sex with another man's wife**, each one of you knowing how to keep your own body in a state of holiness and honor, and not in a state of passion like the Gentiles who don't know God—which means not trying to get around and **cheat your brother in the process**, because when it comes to all such things the Master is the avenger, just as we have told you and testified to before.[270]—Paul

While sex with another man's wife violates Jesus' Law, Paul wrote that everything is lawful in the context of pre-marital sex with prostitutes. There's only one explanation for his overarching message— the Justices. It's time for Christians to accept that Paul dutifully taught that Leviticus 19:18 is Jesus' entire Law, even when it came to idolatry, heterosexuality, and homosexuality.

---

270   1 Thessalonians 4:2-6 as translated by Dr. William Berg

Chapter 35

Lady Stealers

Languages often follow predictable patterns. In English, "singers" are those who sing. "Dancers" are those who dance. "Writers" are those who write. In Greek, *pornoi* are those who engage in *porneia*:

> **Porneia is actually reported among you—the sort of *porneia* that we don't find even among Gentiles—, to the effect that someone is getting in bed with his father's wife.** How can you be so smug about it, instead of raising a complaint so that **the one who did this can be plucked from your midst?**
>
> For you see I, absent in body but present in the Spirit, have already judged, as if present, the man who has done that thing in that manner, and in the name of Master Jesus, whenever you and my spirit are gathered together, I have decided, with the power of our Master Jesus, to hand this sort of man over to Satan for the destruction of his flesh, so that his spirit may be saved on the Day of the Master.
>
> It's not a pretty sight, this feather in your cap! Don't you know that a little yeast makes all the dough rise? **Get rid of the old yeast**, so that you may be new dough, unleavened, just as you are, for the Paschal feast, for our sacrificial lamb is the Messianic King. Then let us hold the feast, not in the old yeast or the yeast of evil and shame, but in unleavened sincerity and truth.
>
> **I told you in the (previous) letter not to associate with *pornoi* ...**[271]

This passage is a critical one for understanding Paul's sexual vocabulary. He starts out by saying that there is a form of having sex

---

271   1 Corinthians 5:1-9

with another man's woman that isn't even found among the Gentiles. This extreme form of *porneia*—this extreme form of having sex with another man's woman—involves a man having sex with his father's wife. Paul commands the Corinthians to cast this man out of their midst, for he told them "in the (previous) letter not to associate with *pornoi*."

When the Judeo-Christian community expanded *porneia* to include *sex involving another man's woman*, it likewise expanded the meaning of *pornoi* to include *those engaged in sex with another man's woman*. In fact, every instance of *pornoi* in the New Testament epistles refers to those engaged in sex with another man's woman. Every single one. This is such a critical distinction that it bears repeating and repeating.

> *Every instance of* pornoi *in the New Testament epistles refers to those engaged in sex with another man's woman.*

We saw that this is the case in the passage above. Another clear example involves Esau, the poster child for raping another man's woman:

> **Esau violated a betrothed maiden** and committed murder[272]—Sander L. Gilman (former professor at Cornell University who later founded the Program in Jewish Studies at the University of Illinois)[273]

> * * *

> Esau committed three abominations–**violating a betrothed maiden**, murder, and theft[274]—Louis H. Feldman (Professor of Classics at Yeshiva University)

> * * *

> For some time Esau had been pursuing his evil inclinations in secret. Finally he dropped his mask, and on the day of Abraham's death he was guilty of five crimes: **he ravished a betrothed maiden**, committed murder, doubted the resurrection of the dead, scorned the birthright, and denied God.—Louis

272 *Anti-Semitism in Times of Crisis* by Sander L. Gilman, Steven T. Katz, p. 111, NYU Press, 1993
273 *Josephus's Interpretation of the Bible* by Louis H. Feldman, p. 316, University of California Press, 1998
274 *Josephus's Interpretation of the Bible* by Louis H. Feldman, p. 316, University of California Press, 1998

Ginzberg (a Talmudist[275] and leading figure in the Conservative Movement of Judaism of the twentieth century)[276]

According to the ancient Jews, Esau raped the betrothed woman right before selling his birthright for a single meal. This timing caused Esau's intercourse with another man's woman to be permanently linked in Jewish minds to the sale of his birthright. The Biblical book of Hebrews presumed this link:

> that there be no *pornoi* or godless person like Esau, who sold his own birthright for a single meal.—Hebrews 12:16

As a reminder, the ancient Jews were convinced that Esau raped the betrothed maiden because of *Gezera Shava*. It is this *Gezera Shava*-discovered rape of another man's woman that provides the key to understanding *pornoi* in Hebrews 12:16:

> that **there be no one who engages in sex with another man's woman** or godless person like Esau, who sold his own birthright for a single meal.

A final example of *pornoi* is found in Hebrews.

> Everyone is to honor marriage and keep the marriage bed undefiled; for *pornoi* and adulterers God will judge.[277]

Here's an interesting question: Why does the author of Hebrews use both *pornoi* and adulterers side by side? Fortunately, we find the exact same pairing in a writing from Justin Martyr:

> What is the accusation? Why do you punish this man, **not as an adulterer, nor as a *pornos* [singular of *pornoi*]**, nor murderer, nor thief, nor robber, nor convicted of any crime whatsoever, but as one who has only professed that he is called by the name Christian?"—Justin Martyr (Early second century Christian author and apologist)[278]

Justin's text tells us everything we need to know. Justin was writing about a man who had wrongfully been brought before the Roman magistrate. Justin is inquiring of his charge. It is crucial to note that neither male prostitution nor sexual promiscuity was illegal

275   Talmudist: a scholar of ancient Jewish law
276   *The Legends of the Jews: From the Creation to Jacob* by Louis Ginzberg, p. 318, Cosimo, Inc., 2006
277   Hebrews 13:4
278   2 Apology 2.16

in the early Roman Empire. However, adultery and having sex with another man's wife was. In other words, even single people who had sex with other people's wives could be charged with a crime. Thus, there is only one possible meaning of *pornoi* in this particular pairing with adulterers: unmarried men who have sex with another man's wife.

This concurs perfectly with the context of the Hebrews passage. The Hebrews passage is discussing "honoring marriage" and keeping it "undefiled". Thus, both Justin's manuscript and the context of Hebrews inform us what the passage actually said:

> Everyone is to honor marriage and keep the marriage bed undefiled; for God will judge unmarried men who sleep with other men's wives and those who are married who are unfaithful to their spouse.[279]

The passage is very simple to understand. It is condemning both unfaithful married folks and anyone unmarried who has sex with them.

How do modern Bibles translate this carefully worded passage?

> Marriage is to be held in honor among all, and the marriage bed is to be undefiled; for **fornicators** and adulterers God will judge.—Hebrews 13:4

Here we go again. Modern conventional Bibles have a very bad habit of launching a tirade against fornication by changing "sex with another man's woman" (which inherently violates Jesus' Law) into "fornication" (which doesn't inherently violate Jesus' Law). Their refusal to give a faithful rendition of the original text creates another red herring. All of these red herrings prevent modern readers from recognizing Paul's flawless commitment to promoting the Law of the Messianic King: "Love your neighbor as yourself."

---

279   Hebrews 13:4

Chapter 36

Setting the Record Straight

One New Testament verse in particular (1 Corinthians 6:9) takes the prize for being so perversely translated that it actually seems to repudiate the Law of the Messianic King. That verse appears to be so anti-Golden Rule that it even causes many liberals to conclude that Paul rejected Leviticus 19:18 as the entire Law. Many liberals believe that they have to choose between Jesus and Paul. But the seeming contradiction is merely an illusion created by disingenuous translators.

Consider 1 Corinthians 6:9 as it is found in the popular NASB Bible:

> Or do you not know that the unrighteous will not inherit the kingdom of God? Do not be deceived; neither fornicators, nor idolaters, nor adulterers, nor effeminate, nor homosexuals

Does fornication inherently violate the Law of the Messianic King? No, it does not. Do idolaters inherently break the Golden Rule? No, they do not. Do effeminate men inherently transgress Leviticus 19:18? No, they do not. Do homosexuals inherently violate the Justices? No, of course not. Well, now we know why humanity is thoroughly convinced that Paul didn't preach the Golden Rule. The sorely mistranslated versions of 1 Corinthians 6:9 tell them so.

Now we've finally come to the crux of the matter. On the one hand, Paul famously wrote:

- Christians are enslaved to a Law that is completely fulfilled in one precept, "Love your neighbor as yourself."[280]

- Bearing each other's burdens fulfills the Law of the Messianic King.

- Christians are not under the Torah, but under the Law of the Messianic King (the Law that we fulfill by bearing each other's burdens).

- God considers anyone who fulfills the Justices of the Torah as having kept the entire Law.

- Only the commandments based on "love your neighbor as yourself" are the Law.

- God will judge people based solely on the altruism of their deeds.[281]

- And so on, and so on.

Yet modern Bibles have the gall to make it appear that Paul took all of this back in a single verse, 1 Corinthians 6:9. In fact, they make it look like he took it back four times over: "fornicators," "idolaters," "effeminate men," and "homosexuals"!

These Bibles preach a very different gospel than Paul's. They've invented a Paul who taught that God had a rule list above and beyond the Golden Rule. Moreover, their mythical Paul has captured the world's imagination. The historical, real-world Paul has been completely discarded in the process.

Let's take a look at their rather inventive list:

- *Idolaters*—Paul chided those who criticized others for eating meat that had been sacrificed to idols. This form of idolatry certainly wasn't a deal breaker for him. Also, Paul refused to forbid his Corinthian converts to dine in idolatrous temples, even though he sorely wanted them to

---

280   See chapter 5, "Terms of Enslavement"
281   See chapter 14, "Paul in a Nutshell"

stop. This form of idolatry wasn't a deal breaker for him, either. There is only one form of idolatry that Paul said will keep a person out of the kingdom of God—greed (worshiping material things).[282] Interestingly, greed is the only form of idolatry condemned by Jesus of Nazareth in his Sermon on the Mount. In Paul's and Jesus' theologies, those who worship material things cannot enter the kingdom of God.

- *Sexually Immoral*—The word that is translated as "fornicators" is *pornoi*. Paul is condemning those who have sex with another man's woman.[283, 284]

- *Effeminate*—The word that is translated as "the effeminate" is *malakoi*. Paul is condemning the self-indulgent.[285]

- *Homosexuals*—The word that is translated as "homosexuals" is *arsenokoitai*. Paul is condemning the rapists of young boys.[286]

It is truly breathtaking how much this one single verse has been changed through mistranslation. It is literally impossible to embrace the mistranslated version of 1 Corinthians 6:9 and also believe that Leviticus 19:18 is the entire Law. It is literally impossible to embrace the mistranslated version of 1 Corinthians 6:9 and to believe Paul's Gospel at the same time.

---

282   Ephesians 5:5

283   See chapter 35, "Lady Stealers" for documentation on the Greek word *pornoi*.

284   The Greek word that Paul used here was *pornoi*. It is rather fortunate that Paul used the word pornoi in 1 Corinthians 5, the chapter right before 1 Corinthians 6:9. This allows us to know with certainty what Paul was referring to when he wrote 1 Corinthians 6:9. In 1 Corinthians 5, Paul discussed excommunicating a man who was having sex with his father's wife. Paul called this a form of *porneia* worse than that which Gentile unbelievers engaged in. [1 Corinthians 5:1] (In other words, he called this a form of taking another man's woman worse than that which the Gentile unbelievers engaged in.) Paul commanded them to oust this man from the church [1 Corinthians 5:2-8], for he had already written to them that they shouldn't associate with *pornoi*. [1 Corinthians 5:9] Here we have an undeniable case of Paul using *pornoi* to reference those who engage in *porneia*, i.e. those who take another man's wife .

In this particular instance, *pornoi* is completely unrelated to prostitution, just as it is also unrelated to premarital promiscuity. Instead, it designates the type of men who take another man's wife, as exemplified by the man who took his father's wife. This is the way Paul used *pornoi* in the very chapter that precedes 1 Corinthians 6:9. This the way all the other epistles used *pornoi* as well (see the previous chapter, "Lady Stealers").

285   See chapter 24, "Indulge Me"

286   See chapter 29, "Decalogue Distinction" and chapter 30, "Lay of the Land"

This is why conservatives balk at the notion that Leviticus 19:18 is the entire Law. Their Bibles have convinced them that it isn't. Their Bibles have convinced them to balk at the very message that the historical Paul dedicated his life to teaching. This is the dilemma we now face.

Chapter 37
Cognitive Dissonance

The Justices and the Jobs weren't mere theoretical, abstract concepts to Paul. On the contrary, the difference between them was very personal.

During Paul's day, the two most popular Pharisaic schools were the School of Hillel and the School of Shammai. Paul was educated in the School of Hillel by Gamaliel—the head of the school and the grandson of Hillel himself:

> I am a Jew, born in Tarsus of Cilicia, but brought up in this city, educated under Gamaliel, according to the strictness of ancestral law, being zealous for God just as you all are today. I persecuted this Way to the death, binding and putting both men and women into prisons—Acts 22:3-4

Christianity used to be known as "the Way." Paul persecuted members of the Way "to the death." What was driving him?

> Now, you've heard about my former conduct in Judaism, the fact that I used to **persecute the assembly of God to excess, and tried to lay it waste**, and so I got ahead in Judaism, beyond many of my contemporaries in the same class, **standing out as especially zealous for my ancestral traditions.**

Paul's drive was his special zeal for his ancestral traditions, a zeal that was even greater than that of his contemporaries. Paul considered Christianity to be a fierce enemy of the ancestral traditions. In other words, Paul considered Christianity to be a fierce enemy of the Jobs.

However, despite Paul's zeal for the Jobs, he found himself

incapable of keeping the Justices. He found himself incapable of keeping the commandment, "do not covet":

> What, then, shall we say? That Torah is sin? Far from it! On the contrary: if not for Torah, I wouldn't have recognized sin, for **I wouldn't have known coveting unless the Torah had said, "Do not covet."** After getting its start through that commandment, **sin activated every coveting in me**; for without the law, sin is dead.—Romans 7:7-8 (trans. Dr. William Berg)

The Torah's commandment "do not covet" made him aware that coveting was sin. Being a zealous person, he doggedly tried to stop coveting. But the more he tried not to covet, the more he coveted:

> the good that I want to do, I don't do; instead, I do the evil that I don't want to do.—Romans 7:19

We must always remember that Paul's struggle with coveting was a struggle with a Justice. He was unable to keep one of the commandments based on "Love your neighbor as yourself."

> he who loves others has fulfilled the Law because "don't commit adultery," "don't murder," "don't steal," **"don't covet," and if there is any other commandment it is summed up in these words: "You shall love your neighbor as yourself."**[287]—Paul

"Do not covet" is a Justice of the Torah. Hence, the Jobs and the Justices were very personal to Paul. While Paul kept the Jobs, he found it impossible to keep the Justices. It is very likely that his inner struggle was what motivated him to lay Christianity to waste. Christians were teaching that only the Justices were the Law. How infuriated (and frightened) Paul must have been. If the Christians were right, then all his zealous effort spent on keeping the Jobs was for nothing. If the Christians were right, then he was still heading for the fire.

Paul wrote that he tried to overcome coveting prior to meeting Jesus. This shows that he was already keenly aware of his problem. He was already keenly aware of the tension between the Justices and the Jobs. This self-awareness made him an ideal canvas for Jesus to paint upon. But before we discuss the work that Jesus did in Paul's heart, we must first understand: *what exactly is coveting?*

---

287   Romans 13:8-9

Chapter 38
Thou Shalt Not Covet

In Paul's day, coveting was not a sexual term. A passage from the ancient Church Father Justin Martyr makes this abundantly clear:

> Let him of no man covet wife or child,
> His splendid house, his wide-spread property,
> His maiden, or his slave born in his house,
> His horses, or his cattle, or his adult cows,
> Nay, covet not a pin, O Pamphilus[288]

Justin certainly wasn't concerned about Pamphilus having sexual desires for the man's house, property, horses, cattle, adult cows, and pin. (One would think that sex with a pin would be quite inconvenient, to say the least.) Justin's passage documents that coveting wasn't a sexual term; it was an *ethical* one. "To covet" meant to want everything for yourself. Coveting referred to selfishness and greed.[289]

People can selfishly and greedily desire even their own belongings, not just their neighbor's. In other words, it is possible for a person to covet his own possessions. The Gospel of Matthew records just such an instance. Jesus tells a rich young ruler to sell all of his possessions and give the resulting money to the poor. The man cannot bring himself to do this, and he walks away from Jesus with great sorrow. Regarding this incident, the ancient Church Father Irenaeus

---

288   *On the Sole Government of God* by Justin Martyr, chapter IV (a second-century Christian writing)
289   See also Ignatius's exhortation against those who are "covetous of other men's possessions, swallowing up wealth insatiably." (*Epistle to the Magnesians* by Saint Ignatius, chapter IX). Ignatius was a contemporary of the apostles and studied under Jesus' disciple, John.

wrote:

> The Lord, **exposing his covetousness,** said to him, "If thou wilt be perfect, go, sell all that thou hast, and distribute to the poor; and come, follow me;" promising to those who would act thus, the portion belonging to the apostles.[290]

The man's desire for his own possessions exceeded his desire to help others. Therefore, Irenaeus wrote that the man coveted his own possessions.

This helps us greatly to understand Paul's pre-conversion struggle. Paul was proud of his zeal for the Jobs of the Torah. Yet he recognized that his desire for material things far exceeded his desire to help others. He realized that, despite his religious zeal, he was a selfish, greedy bastard, and his selfish greed caused him to do a lot of evil things.

Paul's struggle with coveting made him keenly aware of his inability to practice *dikaiosune*. Imagine the guilt he must have felt when he read Jewish writings like this:

> And for all those who **practice *dikaiosune*** from out of your possessions give your alms… Give of your bread to the hungry one, and from your clothing to the naked ones; **make an almsgiving from everything that you have more than enough for you.**[291]

Wanting everything for ourselves is the opposite of sharing our extras with those in need. Coveting is the mirror opposite of practicing *dikaiosune*. In other words, Paul's obsession with trying to fix his own coveting was an obsession with trying to practice *dikaiosune*:

> **the good that I want to do,** I don't do; instead, I do the evil that I don't want to do.—Romans 7:19

When Paul wrote that he tried to do good instead of evil, he wrote this in a passage that contrasted practicing *dikaiosune* to coveting. In Romans 6, Paul told his converts that they must render the members of their body as instruments of *dikaiosune* unto God.[292]

---

290   "Against Heresies," Book IV, by Irenaeus, chapter 12.
291   Tobit 4:6-7, 16
292   Romans 6:12

He even told them that they must be enslaved to *dikaiosune*.[293] Then, in chapter seven, he offered his own previous struggle with coveting as a contrast. Given that coveting is the mirror opposite of practicing *dikaiosune*, his illustrative choice was a perfect one.

So does the story end here? Did Paul always remain a covetous son-of-a-gun? Or did he finally find a way to be emancipated from coveting, and instead, enslaved to practicing *dikaiosune*?

---

293   Romans 6:18

Chapter 39
New Creation

It must have given Paul great joy to be able to honestly proclaim:

> **I have coveted no one's silver or gold or clothes. You yourselves know that these hands ministered to my own needs and to the men who were with me.** In everything I showed you that by working hard in this manner you must help the weak and remember the words of **the Lord Jesus, that He Himself said, "It is more blessed to give than to receive."**[294]

Paul overcame his coveting. Even more surprisingly, he became the opposite of the man he used to be. With gains earned from his own hands, he ministered to the needs of the men who were there with him. Paul worked hard to take care of himself, and then he shared his extras with those who needed it. To paraphrase Paul, "I no longer covet. I practice *dikaiosune* instead."

What changed Paul's life? How did he go from a covetous son-of-a-gun to a person who practiced *dikaiosune* instead? Paul explained the source of his transformation in Romans 8:

> **For the Law of the spirit of the life in Jesus the Messianic King emancipated me from the Law of sin and death. For what the Law was powerlessness to do (in that it was weakened by the flesh), God did** by sending his own son in the likeness of the sinful flesh. And regarding sin he pronounced a sentence on sin in the flesh **that the Law's requirement of justice might be fulfilled in us—the ones who don't behave conforming to the flesh but conforming to the spirit.**

---

294   Acts 20:33-35 NASB

In chapter seven, Paul described himself as a slave to sin. Sin controlled him. It made him covet. Then, in chapter eight, he declared that he was emancipated from the sin of coveting through the Spirit that he received by faith in Jesus. Ever since, by walking in the Spirit, he fulfilled the Law's Justices all the days of his life.

Knowledge of the first-century Justices and Jobs helps us to better understand Paul's conversion to Christianity. Paul used to be a man who kept the Jobs while violating the Justices. This makes Romans 2 one of the most important chapters ever written by Paul.

In Romans 2, Paul chastises fellow Jews who were keeping the Jobs while violating the Justices. (They were acting like Paul did during his pre-Christian days.) It is to these Jews that he said that only those who persist in altruistic deeds will inherit life.[295] It is to these Jews that Paul said that only those who keep the entire Law will be vindicated before God.[296] (And it was to these Jews that he explained: those who keep the Justices will be considered to have kept the whole Law, while those who only keep the Jobs will be considered to have violated the whole Law.)[297] *This was Paul's stern warning to those who lived as he once did: zealous for the Jobs while violating the Justices.*

It is quite unfortunate that Romans 2 has been considered a theological mystery for two millennia, for it may very well be the most essential chapter ever written by Paul. Those who slander homosexuals are violating the Justices. They are committing sin worthy of spiritual death. Meanwhile, the ancient prohibition on adult homosexuality is Job of the Torah; as both the historical record and Paul's careful wording attest. When it comes to homosexuality, many Christians are zealous for a Job of the Torah while they are violating the Justices. They have completely missed Paul's message in Romans 2.

---

295   See chapter 14, "Paul in a Nutshell"
296   Romans 2:13
297   Romans 2:26 (see chapter 22, "Mystery Solved")

Chapter 40

Assurance of Salvation

Paul wanted his converts to test themselves in order to make sure that they were "in the Faith":

> Put yourselves to the test to find out if you are in the Faith; assess yourselves! Or do you not know yourselves that Messianic King Jesus is in you—unless of course you fail the test?[298]

To express his order to "assess" themselves, Paul chose the Greek verb *dokimazo*. Paul used *dokimazo* in another letter in which he wanted his converts to assess themselves:

> **Bear each other's burdens, and in that way fulfill the Messianic King's Law.** For if someone thinks he is something, and is nothing, he deceives himself. **But let each one assess his own performance**[299]

In Paul's theology, knowing whether or not "Jesus is in you" was very simple. If a person bears the burdens of others, then Jesus is in him and he is in the Faith. This, of course, is fully consistent with everything else that Paul wrote. He consistently taught that everyone who keeps the Law of the Messianic King is in the Faith.

Paul's bottom-line theology was simple: If you truly "love your neighbor as yourself," then Jesus must be in you and you are in the Faith. This test can be done by any man or woman, black or white, straight or gay. If a homosexual truly loves his neighbor as himself,

---

298   2 Corinthians 13:5
299   Galatians 6:2-4

then Jesus' spirit must be in him and he is of the Faith. Thus sayeth Paul.

Because the New Testament was written to promote the Law of the Messianic King, this is one principle that all its authors agreed upon. According to John, to believe in Jesus means to "love one another just as he commanded us":

> This is God's commandment: To trust the authority of his son Messianic King Jesus and therefore love one another just as he commanded us.[300]

In John's theology, God has only one commandment: Trust that Jesus knew what he was talking about, and therefore, love one another just as he commanded. This was John's way of teaching that loving your neighbor is the entirety of the Law.

John, like Paul, believed that anyone who kept the Law of the Messianic King must already know God:

> Beloved, let us love one another, for love is from God; and **everyone who loves is born of God and knows God.**[301]

Just like Paul, John believed that *loving others* is a dependable measurement to assess whether or not we are in the Faith:

> We *know* **that we have passed out of death into life,** *because* **we love the brethren.**[302]

Anyone who truly loves others can be fully assured of their salvation. Thus sayeth John.

If a homosexual truly loves others, doesn't he pass the test? According to Paul and John, such a person can have full assurance of their salvation. They can rest assured that they are "born of God and know God." Where is the "God said it; I believe it; and that settles it for me" crowd when it comes to these verses? Is that crowd willing to stand up for what the Bible teaches here?

In Peter's theology, anyone who persists in loving others can be

300   1 John 3:23
301   1 John 4:7-8 NASB
302   1 John 3:14 NASB

sure that his sins are covered, even if he has a multitude of them:

> Most importantly above all else, remain persistent in your love for one another because love covers over a multitude of sins.[303]

Peter, John, and Paul all agreed on what assures a person's salvation: keeping the Law of the Messianic King—"Love your neighbor as yourself."

The Biblical author James taught the same thing too:

> Now **if you are accomplishing the King's Law according to scripture, "You shall love your neighbor as yourself," you are behaving well**.... Speak and act like people who are about to be judged by the Law of freedom; for **merciless judgment is for the one who has not shown compassion. Compassion triumphs over judgment.**

> What good is it, my brothers and sisters, if one says he has faith but doesn't have the deeds? **Such 'faith' isn't able to save that person, is it? If brothers or sisters are there unclothed and lacking their daily bread, and one of you says to them, "Go in peace, stay warm and well-fed," and doesn't give them what their bodies need, what good is that?**[304]

For James, assurance of salvation was really simple: Anyone who follows the King's Law, "Love your neighbor as yourself," is doing well. He will triumph in judgment because of his compassion. James is but one more Biblical author who believed that fulfilling Leviticus 19:18 assures a person's salvation.

What cruel twist of logic now has entire denominations rejecting this clear Biblical teaching when it comes to gays? If a homosexual couple is fulfilling the Law of the Messianic King, then the spirit of Jesus is within them and they are in the Faith. Period. Those who preach otherwise need to be lovingly, yet sternly, educated on what the Bible actually says. They are preaching a different gospel than the one taught by Jesus, John, James, Peter, *and Paul*.

303   1 Peter 4:8
304   James 2:8-16

Chapter 41

Holiness

"What about holiness?" many will ask. "Loving others isn't God's only behavioral standard. God called us to be holy, just as he is holy."

Sounds good on the surface, but does the implication even pass the smell test? For example:

- Did Peter forget about holiness when he wrote that loving others covers over a multitude of sins?

- Did John forget about holiness when he wrote that everyone who loves others is born of God and knows God?

- Did James forget about holiness when he wrote that everyone who shows compassion to others will triumph in judgment?

- Did Paul forget about holiness when he taught that "Love your neighbor as yourself" is the entire Law?

- Did Jesus forget about holiness when he taught that fulfilling Leviticus 19:18 via the Golden Rule is the narrow road to life?

Of course they didn't forget about holiness. They all knew about holiness, and yet, they all taught that loving others gives assurance of salvation at the same time. How can this be? The answer is elusively obvious. There's a one-to-one relationship between love for others and holiness. In Paul's theology, "holiness" and "perfection in loving others" happen to be the very same thing:

> **may the Lord cause you to increase and abound in love for one another, and for all people, just as we also do for you; <u>so that</u> He may establish your hearts without blame in holiness** before our God and Father at the coming of our Lord Jesus with all His saints.[305]

Paul wrote that perfecting our love for others is what produces holiness. They are two sides of the same coin. Now we know why Peter, James, John, Jesus, and Paul all taught what they did about salvation.

Paul likely got his teaching on holiness from Jesus' Sermon on the Mount.

> love your enemies and pray for those who persecute you, so that you may be sons of your Father who is in heaven; for He causes His sun to rise on the evil and the good, and sends rain on the righteous and the unrighteous. For if you love those who love you, what reward do you have? Do not even the tax collectors do the same? If you greet only your brothers, what more are you doing than others? Do not even the Gentiles do the same? Therefore you are to be perfect, as your heavenly Father is perfect.[306]

Jesus taught that those who love everyone, including their enemies, are *perfect*. Let's apply "God said it; I believe it; and that settles it for me." In other words, if a homosexual couple loves everyone, including their enemies, they are *perfect*. Jesus said it. I believe it. That settles it for me.

For Jesus and Paul, holiness comes from loving others. Homosexuality, gay marriage, and the ordination of gay clergy simply aren't holiness issues. Those who say otherwise contradict both Jesus' and Paul's teachings on holiness.

It's time to affirm the holiness of homosexual Christian brothers and sisters who make the needs of others equal to their own through the empowerment of the indwelling Spirit of Christ. It's time to do this because the Bible tells us so.

---

305   1 Thessalonians 3:12-13
306   Matthew 5:44-48 NASB

Chapter 42
If it Ain't Broke

Paul wrote that Christians can be sure of their salvation if they love others through the indwelling Spirit received by faith in Jesus. Such people can rest assured that they have the kind of faith that saves.

This is neither a platitude nor some new-fangled liberal idea. Paul taught this as a practical, real-world theology. Paul's issue with coveting is a perfect example. His religious teachers taught him "do not covet" because the Torah commanded it. Paul desperately wanted to please God. He tried feverishly to stop coveting. But the more effort he exerted, the more he ended up coveting.

Many people today are in a situation that is similar to Paul's. Consider adultery, a major problem in today's Church. When a man comes for counseling, many pastors will say, "The Bible says, 'Do not commit adultery.' Therefore, you must stop it." The husband feverishly tries his best to follow the Bible. This approach often produces one of two outcomes:

- The husband continues committing adultery. However, now he is committing adultery with an extra heap of guilt.

- The man's willpower allows him to refrain from committing adultery, but he internally struggles with it every frustrating day of his life.

Are these the only two options available to Christians? Not

at all! Paul didn't have a constant struggle with coveting after he met Jesus. A careful reading of Romans 7 and 8 shows that he was liberated from coveting when the Spirit wrote Leviticus 19:18 on his heart. As soon as he genuinely loved others from his heart, coveting was no longer a struggle or even an issue. Paul's love for others caused him to *want* to meet their needs. He did so freely and joyfully.

How did Paul make himself a vessel in order for the Spirit to express love for humanity through him? Paul enslaved his mind to God's Law[307]; he enslaved his mind to the Law which is fulfilled in one precept, "Love your neighbor as yourself."[308] When his mind was set on what the Spirit desires, the misdeeds of the body were automatically put to death.[309] No ongoing struggle. No ongoing frustration. No ongoing sin. Only love, joy, and peace (and all the other fruits of the Spirit, as well.)[310]

When a modern man is unable to remain faithful to his wife, the last thing he needs is a lecture. What he needs is instruction on how to set his mind on what the Spirit desires, and the adultery will disappear on its own. No struggling. No guilt. No sin. Only love, joy, and peace of mind. Many meditations and contemplations exist to assist in nurturing love for spouses and others. Once the husband loves his wife as himself, he will *want* to protect his wife's emotions and he will *want* to protect her health as well. It becomes a joy to do that for her. (Furthermore, he grows in faith and becomes closer to God, as well.)

Churches will be overflowing with new congregants if they can only orient themselves to this practical application of Paul's teaching of love, love, love. Paul wasn't naïve. On the contrary, he knew that it's the only thing that really works. Every spiritual imperfection is healed by one remedy: "Love your neighbor as yourself."

Will growing in love stop a person from committing adultery? Of course! Will growing in love stop a person from stealing? Of course! Will growing in love stop a person from murdering? Of course!

307   Romans 7:25
308   Romans 13:8-9, Galatians 5:14
309   Romans 8:6, 12-13
310   Galatians 5:22

What about minor imperfections, such as jealousy and strife? Will growing in love stop a person from being jealous? Of course! As love grows, we genuinely rejoice in the amazing things that other people receive in life. Will growing in love stop a person from causing strife? Of course! As we grow in love, we do everything in our power to assist other people in having a joyful, peaceful time. It becomes our pleasure to do so.

Everything that is contrary to God is automatically remedied as a person grows in love for others. This is why Paul taught that holiness results from loving others.

Now here is the million-dollar question: Will homosexuals stop being gay as they grow in love for others? From a Biblicist perspective, this is the single most important question that we can ask about this issue.

The color of a person's eyes is completely independent of his level of love for others. A person's gender is completely independent of his level of love for others. A person's sexual orientation is completely independent of his level of love for others. Eye color, gender, and sexual orientation have nothing to do with spirituality. *A person who is perfected in love will still have the same eye color, gender, and sexual orientation.*

This is not a hypothesis or a theory. It's a natural law that's been proven after decades of conversion therapy experiments. Exodus International has been offering its services to teach gay people how to become straight for 35 years. After three and a half decades, this is what they now say:

> "In the 1980's and '90s, the counseling emphasis was heavier than it was today," said Alan Chambers, the president of Exodus. "Transformation in Christ is possible, but **it doesn't necessarily mean that we will never be tempted or completely move beyond a certain struggle that we may have.**"[311]

---

[311] "Amid Bachmann controversy, many Christians cool to conversion therapy for gays" Religion blogs, by Dan Gilgoff, CNN.com Religion Editor, reported on July 18, 2011, CNN religion blogs, http://religion.blogs.cnn.com/2011/07/18/amid-bachmann-controversy-many-christians-cool-to-conversion-therapy-for-gays/

What a cruel, destructive, anti-Biblical theological perspective. There is a reason why homosexuals still "struggle" with their homosexuality. There was nothing wrong with them in the first place. That's why love doesn't liberate them from it. People who graduate from Exodus International live the rest of their days struggling within themselves, instead of finding the peace which transcends all understanding. That's the sad result of anti-Paul theology.

Paul wasn't left to struggle with coveting all the days of his life. Love for others liberated him from it. That's how it works.

The Spirit's sole function is to write the Law of brotherly love on the human heart. *If loving others doesn't fix something, then it was never broken in the first place.* That's why loving others doesn't "fix" eye color, gender, or sexual orientation. These aren't spiritual deficiencies to begin with. Thus, "If it ain't broke, don't try to fix it!"

In their rejection of Paul's message, many denominations are irreversibly harming the homosexual minority group. A recent study of 34 counties in Oregon found that gay teenagers living in less tolerant counties are more likely to commit suicide than those who live in liberal ones. It's intuitive that this would be the case. Now the numbers confirm it. Twenty-five percent of gay teenagers in the least tolerant counties attempt to end their lives.[312] It should be noted that political affiliation was one of the measures used to assess county tolerance. The more conservative counties were the ones associated with an increase in suicides. (It's also worth noting that conservative counties experienced a 9% increase in suicides of straight teens as well.)[313]

When will Christians wake up to the idea that conservative Christian districts should be the most tolerant, supportive environments? Gay teen suicides in Bible-believing districts should be virtually unheard of. What a testimony about Jesus that would be!

---

312   "Suicide risk jumps for gay teens in 'unsupportive' counties" by Neil Katz, reported on April 18, 2011, CBS News, http://www.cbsnews.com/8301-504763_162-20054864-10391704.html, September 1, 2011

313   "Suicide risk jumps for gay teens in 'unsupportive' counties" by Neil Katz, reported on April 18, 2011, CBS News, http://www.cbsnews.com/8301-504763_162-20054864-10391704.html, September 1, 2011

Imagine if the world realized that everywhere Christianity abounded, gay teen suicide rates were significantly lower or even non-existent. People would recognize the disciples of Jesus by their love.

But the anti-Biblical perspective towards homosexuals is currently amplifying intolerance, resulting in disastrous consequences at the hands of the mentally unstable and morally weak:

> Ms. Greene interviewed more than 400 young men incarcerated for gay-bashing, and scrutinized their case studies. In an interview published in The Boston Globe this spring, she said she found that **the gay-bashers generally saw nothing wrong in what they did, and, more often than not, said their religious leaders and traditions sanctioned their behavior.** One convicted teen-age gay-basher told her that the pastor of his church had said, "Homosexuals represent the devil. Satan," and that the Rev. Jerry Falwell had echoed that charge.—the late Peter Gomes (former Professor of Christian Morals, Harvard University)[314]

The studies show that the demonization of homosexuals produces two lethal effects:

- It causes a significant percentage of homosexual teens to take their own lives.

- It causes unstable individuals to murder homosexuals.

Sadly, instead of Christianity being a buffer against such horrific results, it is currently a potent instigator of them. This is now a documented fact, and Christians must come to terms with it.

When gay teenagers are rejected by their blood relations, there should be a dozen churches in the community that those teens can turn to for the unconditional love and support that is missing in their lives. *That* will be a testimony to Jesus.

The reason the Faith doesn't shine today is because many denominations have flatly rejected Paul's message: Christians are to be enslaved to a Law which is fulfilled in one precept, "Love your neighbor as yourself." The Bible-believing Christianity of today is completely missing its opportunity with the gay issue. It should be

314   *The Columbia Reader on Lesbians and Gay Men in Media, Society, and Politics* by James D. Woods, p. 138, Columbia University Press, 1999

on the front lines teaching the secular world that the only thing that matters is faith expressing itself through love.[315] They should be the first in line to proclaim that any gay person who truly loves others through the indwelling Spirit of Christ is absolutely *perfect*—and to proclaim that the same goes for his life-partner, too!

---

315   Galatians 5:6

Chapter 43
Return to Galatia

It's important to pay attention to Paul's tone when reading his letters. Paul told the prostitution-loving Corinthians that pre-marital sex with prostitutes *is lawful*.[316] To the Corinthians who dined in pagan temples, he said, "Hear me out and decide for yourselves if you agree with me." Notice how softly he spoke to them. But to the Galatians, he screamed, "You will fall from grace, be severed from Jesus, and Jesus will no longer be of any benefit to you." Out of all the letters we have from Paul, his letter to the Galatians was the most scathing, by far.

What sin were the *Christian* Galatians committing to earn Paul's greatest condemnation?

Was it idolatry? Nope.

Was it prostitution? Nope.

Was it adultery? Nope.

Was it homosexuality? Nope.

Was it raping boys? Nope.

Some Jews had persuaded the Galatians that they must keep some of the Jobs of the Torah (such as circumcision, feast observances, etc.). This was what had earned the Galatians Paul's most scathing criticism:

---

316   1 Corinthians 6:12. Note that in the context of pre-marital sex with prostitutes, Paul says, "all things are lawful."

> The Messianic King made us free to live in freedom; stand, then, and don't put on the yoke of slavery again.
>
> Look: I, Paul, am telling you that **if you get yourselves circumcised, the Messianic King will be of no use to you. I bear witness again to every man who is being circumcised, that he is now under obligation to keep the entire Torah. You have been cut off from the Messianic King, you seekers of vindication through the Torah; you have fallen from grace.**
>
> For in the Spirit, we, out of faith, eagerly await a hope of justice, fairness and altruism. Because in the Messianic King Jesus neither circumcision nor uncircumcision has any value; but rather faith operating through love does....
>
> **you are enslaved to each other through love because the whole law is fulfilled in one statement: "You will love your neighbor as yourself."**[317]

It is rather unfortunate that conventional Bibles mistranslate Galatians 5:13, causing this passage to be terribly misconstrued. As a reminder, Paul wrote:

> you are **enslaved** to each other through love **because** the whole law is fulfilled in one statement: "You will love your neighbor as yourself." [318]

Enslavement *because of the Law* is enslavement *to the Law*. In other words, this passage is not contrasting the Torah versus "no law whatsoever," as modern Bibles make it appear. On the contrary, the passage is contrasting the Torah with the Law of the Messianic King—"the Law which is fulfilled in one precept, 'Love your neighbor as yourself.'"

> you are enslaved to each other through love because the whole law is fulfilled in one statement: "You will love your neighbor as yourself...." Bear one another's burdens and thereby fulfill the Law of the Messianic King.[319]

The real-world, historical Paul reserved his harshest condemnation for Christians who were adding Jobs of the Torah on top of the Law of the Messianic King. Why did this earn them the harshest condemnation? How could it not! Jesus taught that only the commandments based on Leviticus 19:18—only the Justices—are

---

317   Galatians 5:1-6, 13-14 as translated by Dr. William Berg
318   Galatians 5:13-14 as translated by Dr. William Berg
319   Galatians 5:13-14, 6:2 as translated by Dr. William Berg

the Law; the Jobs are not. Therefore, anyone who embraces even a single Job flatly rejects Jesus' most fundamental teaching. It is literally the opposite of having faith in Jesus. Such folks are saying, "I do not believe you, Jesus, when you say that Leviticus 19:18 is the entire Law." That's why Paul wrote that they will "fall from grace, be severed from Jesus, and Jesus will no longer be of any benefit to them."

Paul told the Galatians that *anyone who believes in even one Job of the Torah is cut off from Jesus and obligated to obey the entire Torah.* That is the danger in insisting on even one single Job of the Torah. Now here's a news flash:

The Old Testament prohibition against homosexuality is a Job of the Torah.

Whenever modern Christians try to use Leviticus against adult homosexuality, they are committing the very same error that earned Paul's harshest condemnation: "You will fall from grace, be severed from Jesus, and Jesus will no longer be of any benefit to you." How can it be any other way? Jesus taught that fulfilling Leviticus 19:18 via the Golden Rule has replaced the Torah as the way to life.[320] Christians who use Leviticus against homosexuals are saying, "No, Jesus. I don't believe you." They have forsaken the faith that saves.

---

320   See chapter 8, "Detour"

Chapter 44

Long Road Home

If someone had told me ten years ago that I would be writing books revealing the true historical background of Christianity, I would have laughed. I assumed that Christianity already had a solid understanding of the history behind the Faith. But, as with many findings, the impetus for all this began with an accidental discovery.

As the teenage son of an evangelical pastor, I had a love affair with the Bible. I couldn't get enough. I even won awards for memorizing entire Biblical books, word for word. One of the books I memorized was Paul's letter to the Romans.

Memorizing Biblical books turned out to be a double-edged sword. As an adult, I became a cryptographer, an expert in a field that requires every piece to fit neatly together with all the other pieces. Looking at things from that cryptanalytic perspective, I found myself deeply troubled by the many contradictions contained in the version of Romans that I had memorized. While my Christian friends simply shrugged them off and went on with their day, I simply couldn't accept the blatant inconsistencies. The inconsistency of Romans 2:13 and 3:20 was high on my list:

The doers of the law will be justified

* * *

By the works of the law no one will be justified

In evangelical Protestantism, Paul's statement that the doers of the Law will be justified is troubling. After all, he appears to be stating that deeds can lead to salvation. How do evangelical theologians deal with this? John Calvin, the founder of Baptist theology, gives the typical evangelical explanation of this statement:

> Still more, **we can prove from this passage that no one is justified by works**; for if they alone are justified by the law who fulfill the law, it follows that no one is justified; **for no one can be found who can boast of having fulfilled the law.**[321]

I have read more than a dozen evangelical commentators parroting the same concept: No one can be found who can boast of having fulfilled the Law. So what's the problem with this? Right after Paul states that the doers of the Law will be vindicated, *he then gives an example of those who are successfully doing the Law:*

> with God, those who simply hear the Law are not vindicated. Rather the doers of the law are the ones who will be vindicated. **For example when gentiles who don't have the law do naturally what the law requires, those gentiles without the law are the law unto themselves.** They are demonstrating the performance of the law written on their hearts[322]

So how did John Calvin deal with the fact that his explanation of Romans 2:13 contradicts the very next sentence? He didn't deal with it. He ignored it. It is mind-boggling that Calvin claims Romans 2:13 *proves* his theology when the very next sentence flatly contradicts what he wrote. His confidence far exceeded his competence in this particular instance.

I was somewhat more heartened to learn that many of today's greatest Biblical scholars acknowledge that no one had been able to reconcile Romans 1–3 over the last two thousand years:

> Paul's statements about the law sometimes seem to contradict one another. As an example, Paul in Romans 3:20 stated that no one can be declared righteous by observing the law, whereas Romans 2:13 seems to state just the opposite.... **The debate on Paul's view of the law is far from finished and promises to continue for a long time to come.**—John B. Polhill (professor of New Testament at Southern Baptist Theological Seminary. He is the

---

321   *Commentaries on the Epistle of Paul to the Romans* by John Calvin, p. 96, Kessinger Publishing, 2006
322   Romans 2:13-14

author of the Acts volume in the New American Commentary.)[323]

* * *

The interpretation of Romans 1:18-3:20 has been notoriously difficult for almost every commentator. Problems begin to take form when one attempts to identify exactly who is being talked about or addressed in the passage…. **Earlier interpreters such as Origen, Jerome, Augustine, and Erasmus wrestled with this issue, and it continues to plague commentators today….**

No one being able to be declared righteous by observing the law (Romans 3:20) is clear, [yet] there are four texts in Romans 2 that seem to espouse a theology of salvation by works or by obedience to the Mosaic Law.[324]— Richard N. Longenecker (Distinguished Professor of New Testament B.A., M.A. Wheaton College; Ph.D. New College, University of Edinburgh)

While I admired their candor and intellectual honesty, I was left with an empty feeling. I realized that if the beginning of Romans couldn't be understood, how in the world could anyone have confidence that the rest of it was interpreted correctly? Certainly the rest of the letter depends on the foundation laid down in the beginning. Yet preachers and theologians acknowledge the mystery of Romans 1–3, and then proceed to teach their own ideas about the letter anyway. As for me, I left the church and Christianity. I didn't want any part in this mental gamesmanship.

I became familiar with sites such as EvilBible.com and SkepticsAnnotatedBible.com because I too had concluded that the Bible was a bunch of self-contradictory, useless, ridiculous nonsense.

The journey back to Christianity was a long one. Or, I should say, the journey to finding authentic Christianity for the first time was a long one. The first step started quite by accident. One day, I was visiting my parents. Romans 2:26 happened to be on the computer screen in my dad's home office:

So if the uncircumcised man keeps the requirements of the Law, will not his uncircumcision be regarded as circumcision?

---

323   *Paul and His Letters* by John B. Polhill, pp. 296-297, B&H Publishing Group, 1999
324   *Studies in Paul, exegetical and theological* by Richard N. Longenecker, p. 98, Sheffield Phoenix Press, 2004

"This is one of the dumbest, self-contradictory statements in the Bible," I mused to myself. "How can an uncircumcised man be keeping all the requirements of a Law that requires circumcision?"

It was in that moment that an incredible epiphany came over me. It dawned on me that I had never memorized the book of Romans. I had only memorized what other people claimed to be the book of Romans. Did Paul really write such a dumb, self-contradictory statement? Paul seemed too eloquent and articulate to have actually written such a ridiculous thing. So the question got under my skin.

The moment I returned home from the 5 ½ hour drive, I began researching Romans 2:26 in Greek. That's the very moment when I fell down the rabbit hole.

Paul didn't write about Gentiles who keep all the requirements of the Law. Rather, he wrote about Gentiles who keep the *dikaiomata* of the Law. "The *dikaiomata* must be a specific group of commandments," I reasoned, "not the whole Law." I was desperate to understand exactly what the *dikaiomata* were. (Yes, cryptographers get desperate to resolve incongruence. We simply cannot live with inconsistencies!)

Realizing that *dikaiomata* belongs to the same word group as *dikaiosune*, I cross-referenced all of Paul's statements involving this word group, and the answer hit me. Paul, more often than not, used that word group to express "the equitable treatment of others." In that moment, Romans 2:26 made perfect sense. *Paul was talking about all the requirements of the Law that are based on the equitable treatment of others.* In other words, Romans 2:26 was saying:

> If the uncircumcised man keeps all the Law's requirements based on the equitable treatment of others, won't his uncircumcision be regarded as circumcision?

The sentence not only didn't contradict itself (which is always nice), but it actually made perfect sense. In order to explain my finding, I developed a shorthand notation (developing shorthand notations is second nature to the mathematically inclined). I determined that Paul treated the Law as if it contained two distinct groups of commandments:

- *Equity-based commandments*—Commandments based on the equitable treatment of others.

- *Non-equity-based commandments*—Commandments that are not based on the equitable treatment of others.

Using this shorthand, I concluded that Romans 2:26 says:

If the uncircumcised man keeps the equity-based requirements of the Law, won't his uncircumcision be regarded as circumcision?

In the Torah, equity-based requirements were commands such as "Don't murder," "Don't steal," and "Don't commit adultery." Non-equity-based requirements were commands such as "Get circumcised," "Observe the Sabbath," and "Don't eat shellfish." As I reflected on the differences between the two groups, it dawned on me:

Romans 2:26 is saying that anyone who keeps the equity-based commandments will be regarded as having kept the non-equity-based commandments too. In this way, they are the ones who will be regarded as having kept the entire Law.

Paul wrote Romans to teach that only the equity-based commandments matter; the non-equity-based commandments don't matter at all. In the blink of an eye, by accident, I had inadvertently answered the 2,000-year-old paradox. As a reminder, the paradox is as follows:

The doers of the law will be justified

* * *

By the works of the law no one will be justified

The answer turned out to be very simple.

Romans 2:13-26 boils down to the following:

The doers of the equity-based requirements will be vindicated before God.

So what about the Romans 3:20?

By the works of the law no one will be justified

The "works of the law" *must* refer to the non-equity-based requirements. The phrase has to mean this. It's the only way for Paul to not have written a contradictory statement. With this realization, the rest of the 2,000-year-old mystery was solved! Romans 3:20 was saying:

By the non-equity-based commandments, no one will be vindicated in God's sight.

In essence, Paul wrote:

Those who keep the equity-based requirements will be vindicated

* * *

By the non-equity-based requirements, no one will be vindicated

Romans 2:13 and 3:20 were actually two sides of the very same coin. They both teach the exact same thing. Not only are they not contradictory, but they have always been restatements of each other.

The moment that I realized the 2,000-year mystery regarding Romans 2:13 and 3:20 was solved, I also realized that these verses taught the same thing Jesus did. Jesus taught that the Golden Rule is the entire Law. In other words, he taught that: *Only the equity-based commandments—only the commandments based on the equitable treatment of others—are the Law.* Not only was Romans 1–3 reconciled, but the reconciliation flawlessly aligned Paul's teaching with Jesus' famous Sermon on the Mount, another historic achievement.

Inspired by these revelations, I dug deep into the Greek and came to three realizations:

1. Jesus and Paul treated the Torah as if it were divided into equity-based commandments and non-equity-based ones. (They didn't treat the Torah as if it was one indivisible entity, as conventional Bibles presume.)

2. Jesus and Paul often used *dikaiosune* to express "the equitable treatment of others" (not "moral righteousness," as conventional Bibles claim).

3. Jesus taught that "Love your neighbor as yourself" is the same as "Love God with your whole being." (He didn't teach that "Love your neighbor as yourself" is like "Love God with your whole being," as modern conventional Bibles claim.)[325]

I wrote *The Jesus Secret* to demonstrate how these three realizations cause the entire New Testament to fit together seamlessly, fluidly, without contradiction. By taking a cryptanalytic approach to the Bible, I had solved the 2,000-year Romans 1–3 mystery and reconciled Paul's writings to Jesus' Sermon on the Mount to boot.

I recognized that a cryptanalytic solution was never going to be accepted by Biblical scholars as sufficient independent proof. Although *The Jesus Secret* contained the first congruent translation of the Bible into English, I fully recognized that I needed to meet Biblical scholars on their own turf. I recognized that they would require historical documentation of each of the cryptanalytic findings. So, after publishing *The Jesus Secret*, I went outside of my cryptographic comfort zone and took a deep dive into first-century language, culture, and law.

As I dug deeper into first-century history, I learned that the ancient Jewish people divided their law into two groups: commandments between man and man, and commandments between man and God. I further learned that the division was demarcated based on Leviticus 19:18—"Love your neighbor as yourself." Bingo! This was the equity-based and non-equity-based division that I knew must have existed based on the cryptanalysis. I now had the historical documentation to explain why Jesus and Paul referred to two separate groups of commandments. They did so because that was the standard division of the Law during their day.

Encouraged by this, I then researched the ancient Jewish

---

325   See above, p. 37 & note.

use of *dikaiosune*. During this phase, I learned that the Septuagint used *dikaiosune* to express the ultimate forms of equitable treatment: altruism and loving kindness. Jesus and Paul both quoted from the Septuagint. Much of their religious vocabulary was based upon it. The historical record had confirmed the second part of the cryptanalysis.

The final phase of research involved examining the ancient Jewish perspective on the two great love commandments: "Love your neighbor as yourself" and "Love God with your whole being." It was during this phase that I learned about the ancient Jewish use of *Gezera Shava*. Because of *Gezera Shava*, Jesus had to have taught that "Love your neighbor as yourself" is the same as "Love God with your whole being."³²⁶ The historical record fully confirmed the third and final part of my original cryptanalysis.

All three cryptanalytic discoveries were now historically documented. The three hypotheses discussed in *The Jesus Secret* were now established historical facts:

- *Jesus and Paul treated the Torah as if it were divided into equity-based commandments and non-equity-based ones.*

  o The ancient Jewish nation divided the Torah into two groups: commandments between man and man, and commandments between man and God. The division was demarcated based on Leviticus 19:18—"Love your neighbor as yourself."

---

326   Matthew 22:39 uses the Greek word homoia combined with *Gezera Shava* to show that the second commandment is identical to the first. Dr. Berg's note: The adjective *homoios* (feminine *homoia*, neuter *homoion*) derives from *homos*, which means "one and the same" (see H. Frisk, *Griechisches etymologisches Wörterbuch* and P. Chantraine, *Dictionnaire etymologique de la langue grecque*, under the ὁμός-entries); *homoios*, likewise, signifies identity at one end of its spectrum of meaning, and similarity at the other end. For the most part, especially in first-century contexts, it leans toward the "upper" end of the spectrum, indicating equivalence, equality, congruence or the "perfect match." Its real force is best seen in Greek mathematics, from Euclid through Archimedes and Ptolemy and beyond, where congruent angles, triangles, polygons, etc. are called *isa kai homoia* ("equal and the same," "one and the same"). In that very common expression, *homoia* reinforces and emphasizes the equality specified in *isa* (the conventional translation, "equal and similar," fails to take note of that intensifying function). (For references, see Liddell-Scott-Jones, Greek Lexicon, under the entry ὅμοιος.) The fact that Matthew 22:37-40 uses *homoia* in the context of a *Gezera Shava* ("equivalent pronouncement") would indicate a semantic position in the upper reaches of homoios' range of meaning, in the area of "equal" or "equivalent," or "the same." Therefore, the Greek text would support the premise that "Love your neighbor as yourself" is one and the same with "Love God with your whole being."

In other words, the ancient Jews divided the commandments into equity-based and non-equity-based commandments, just as the cryptanalysis revealed.

- *Jesus and Paul often used* dikaiosune *to express "the equitable treatment of others."*

  o The Septuagint used *dikaiosune* to express the ultimate forms of equitable treatment: altruism and loving kindness. This finding added a further level of depth to that which the cryptanalysis had already revealed.

- *Jesus taught that "Love your neighbor as yourself" is the same as "Love God with your whole being."*

  o The commandments to "Love God" and "Love your neighbor as yourself" were the only ones to have used the Hebraic form of "You shall love." Thus, via *Gezera Shava*, "Love your neighbor as yourself" is the same as "Love God with your whole being." The historical use of *Gezera Shava* confirmed what the cryptanalysis had already revealed.

Now that the historical record confirmed my cryptanalytic solution, I knew the Biblical code had truly been broken. Therefore, I wrote *Breaking the Romans Code* to demonstrate how the cryptanalysis and historical documentation work together to fully explain the entire book of Romans from beginning to end. I also documented how the cryptanalysis and historical documentation work together to demonstrate how Paul's letter to the Romans is perfectly aligned with Jesus' Sermon on the Mount.

After producing the first complete reconciliation of Romans in 2,000 years, I sought to understand more about the historical Paul. I had caught the history bug and wanted to develop a complete portrait of the real-world man. However, developing such a portrait was outside of my skill set. Fortunately, my initial foray into answering these questions caused me to cross paths with Dr. William Berg (PhD Classical Studies, Princeton University).

During his retirement from teaching Greek and Roman Classics at Stanford, UCLA, and other institutions, Dr. Berg donates his expertise by assisting others with ancient Greek translation at www.translatum.gr. He graciously agreed to serve as a consultant on my historical investigation into Paul's writings. This current work, *Paul on Homosexuality*, is the result of the historical and grammatical research conducted in consultation with Dr. Berg.

Our historical investigation has shown that Paul belonged to the Jewish school of thought that expected the Messianic King to replace the Torah with a Law of his own. Paul, therefore, considered himself to be no longer under Torah, but under the Law of the Messianic King instead. His theology developed around his view of Jesus' life, death, and resurrection. His central-most theology can be summarized as follows:

- During his life, Jesus repeatedly taught that Leviticus 19:18 is the entire Law.

- Through his death, Jesus secured the atonement for our previous violations of Leviticus 19:18.

- Through his resurrection, Jesus made available the living Spirit of Christ to write Leviticus 19:18 on the human heart, empowering those who walk in the Spirit to fulfill Leviticus 19:18 all the days of their lives.

In Paul's theology, a person was saved by believing in the precept of the Messianic King,[327] dying to past sins,[328] and fulfilling the Law's Justices by walking in the Spirit from that day forth.[329] All his other teachings, including his teachings about idolatry and sexuality, revolved around this core.

---

327   "Faith comes from hearing, and hearing by the Messianic King's statement."—Romans 10:17 as translated by Dr. William Berg

328   "For the person who dies has been vindicated from sin."—Romans 6:7 as translated by Dr. William Berg

329   Romans 8:4-5

But doesn't the Church already know what Paul taught? It's time to face the eight-hundred-pound gorilla in the room. The Church's inability to solve Romans 1–3 for the last 2,000 years has always been empirical evidence that the Church didn't understand Paul.

Actually, more than one eight-hundred-pound gorilla occupies the ecclesiastical room. For the last 2,000 years, theologians have struggled to reconcile Paul's teachings on faith with Jesus' Sermon on the Mount, which upheld the need to keep the Law. The Church's struggle to reconcile Paul with Jesus' Sermon on the Mount has also been empirical evidence that Paul has been sorely misunderstood for almost 2,000 years.

An additional family of eight-hundred-pound gorillas are the self-contradictory English translations of Paul's letters—in both Catholic and Protestant Bibles alike. All modern conventional Bibles have Paul declaring that "'Love your neighbor as yourself' is the entire Law"—and yet, "No homosexual shall enter the kingdom of God." Huh? All modern conventional Bibles have Paul declaring that only the commandments based on Leviticus 19:18 are the Law; however, they also have him saying that anyone who violates the commandment against idolatry cannot enter the kingdom of God. Say what? All modern conventional Bibles have Paul declaring that "bearing the burdens of others fulfills the Law of the Messianic King"; however, "No sexually immoral person shall enter the kingdom of God." And so on, and so on. One contradiction follows another.

The self-contradictory translations, the struggle to reconcile Paul with Jesus' Sermon on the Mount, and the unsolved mystery of Romans 1–3 loudly testified that something was amiss in the Church's understanding of Paul. Ironically, that misunderstanding, now two millennia old, boils down to only one mistake: The non-Jewish Christians didn't know that Paul was raised in a culture that divided the Torah into two separate groups of commandments demarcated by Leviticus 19:18. The moment a person realizes this, everything falls neatly and perfectly into place. Romans 1–3 reads seamless and fluidly, devoid of contradiction. Paul's teachings on faith are perfectly aligned with Jesus' teachings on the Law in his Sermon on the Mount. Moreover, as our latest investigation shows, all of Paul's writings can be translated into English without even the slightest hint of incongruence or contradiction.

The modern conservative/liberal schism over homosexuality shines a spotlight on the damage that results from this long-term mischaracterization of the apostle Paul. Paul's writings are wrongly used to convince millions of people to vote against full equality for the homosexual minority in American society. American Christianity has become enthralled with a fictitious, mythical version of Paul. Modern Christians are fervently following erroneous translations which betray the actual man of history.

The historical, real-world Paul would have been the first to concede that homosexual Christians can be *perfectly* holy, provided they are truly bearing the burdens of others and thereby fulfilling the Law of the Messianic King. Paul would have been the first to concede that gay marriage has nothing to do with "Love your neighbor as yourself," and therefore, has nothing to do with a person's spirituality or standing before God. Paul adjusted all his views regarding sexuality, and even idolatry, to match Jesus' most central teaching: Anyone who fulfills Leviticus 19:18 via the Golden Rule is on the narrow road that leads to life. Jesus and Paul really meant *anyone*, whether male or female, black or white, straight or gay.

This is a great day and age for homosexuals. The mischaracterization of Paul's writings has been the greatest obstacle for this minority group to be fully accepted and allowed to enjoy every aspect of a free society. Once the Christian community learns what Paul actually wrote, the barrier to full equality can be torn down once and for all. The world will be a much better place for it.

Chapter 45

Easy as 1, 2, 3

In this work, we have taken a journey together through many twists and turns, and perhaps the amount of information revealed seems overwhelming. Fortunately, the whole gist of it boils down to three simple concepts:

1. The Justices of the Torah were the legal commandments based on Leviticus 19:18—"Love your neighbor as yourself."

2. The Jobs of the Torah were the legal commandments that weren't based on Leviticus 19:18.

3. Paul's teachings on idolatry, heterosexuality, and homosexuality all derived from the presumption that only the Justices are the Law; the Jobs are not.

That's it. It truly is as easy as 1, 2, 3.

Paul was reared in a culture that considered the Justices and the Jobs to be the fundamental division of the Law. From a historical perspective, it is no wonder why all his letters are framed around them. The difference between the Justices and the Jobs is the basis of his discussions on jealousy, anger, strife, drunkenness, idolatry, heterosexuality, homosexuality, and even salvation (vindication before God). The difference between the Justices and the Jobs were the basis of *everything* he wrote.

The Justices Explain *All* of Paul's Writings

	Non-Violation of Justices is a non-mortal offense	Violation of Justices is a mortal offense
Jealousy	1 Corinthians 3:1-3	Galatians 5:19-21
Strife	1 Corinthians 3:1-3	Galatians 5:19-21
Anger	Ephesians 4:26	Galatians 5:19-21
Drunkenness	Ephesians 5:18	Galatians 5:19-21
Idolatry	1 Corinthians 10:14-30	1 Corinthians 6:9
Opposite Gender Sex	1 Corinthians 6:12-13	1 Corinthians 6:9
Same Gender Sex	Romans 1:26-32	1 Corinthians 6:9

The *Greek* texts of the above passages show that all of Paul's teachings are constructed around the Justices of the Torah. Therefore, it's not surprising that those who never knew the Justices and the Jobs misunderstood everything that Paul wrote. They had to. They didn't know the foundational premise of his letters; which is why critical passages, such as Romans 1:18-3:20, remained unresolved for almost 2,000 years. And that's also why conventional Bibles continue to translate large swaths of Paul's writings in a self-contradictory manner.

There needs to be a mass education in the Christian community regarding the Justices and the Jobs. The entire New Testament presumes that the reader is already familiar with them. It is the lack of knowledge regarding the Justices and the Jobs that has resulted in the emergence of numerous denominations and various interpretations of the Bible. Yet knowledge of the historical Justices and Jobs reveals that the New Testament has surprisingly little interpretive latitude. All of the New Testament writers were expressing one singular teaching (each in their own unique way): Only the Justices are the Law; the Jobs are not.

It cannot be emphasized enough that the Justices and the Jobs are not a theological notion. Rather, they are a historical fact. It is equally a fact that Jesus', James', and Paul's references to the Old Testament commandments based on Leviticus 19:18 were all references to the historical Justices of the Torah.[330]   In all of their references, all three of them declared that the Justices were the entire Law.[331]   This was the unifying message that launched the Christian Faith.

The original Jewish prohibition on homosexuality wasn't based on Leviticus 19:18. It was a purity issue. It was a Job of the Torah. Those who condemn homosexuality on religious grounds need to be made aware of the original basis of the Faith.   They need to be made aware of the Justices and the Jobs, and they need to know what Jesus, James, and Paul taught about them.   An education regarding the historical meanings of Biblical terminology will not only affect the Christian view on homosexuality, but it is bound to impact the Christian view on every social issue confronting the world today.   The discovery of the historical demarcation of the Justices and Jobs holds within it the potential to cause a paradigm shift to occur within Christianity, after 2,000 years.

Yes, it's a bold claim to state that Christianity has misunderstood the teachings of Paul for the last 2,000 years. Yet the claim is rooted in documented, verifiable facts. Learning the truth of what Paul wrote needn't be a bad thing. Quite the contrary, it can be a wonderful event for the Christian Faith. For it turns out that the apostle Paul truly believed that loving our neighbors as ourselves was the entirety of the Christian legal obligation. What could be more beautiful than that?

---

330   Jesus referenced the Old Testament commandments based on Leviticus 19:18 in Matthew 19:16-19. Paul referenced the Old Testament commandments based on Leviticus 19:18 in Romans 13:9. James referenced the Old Testament commandments based on Leviticus 19:18 in James 2:8-11. (Note: The prohibitions against showing partiality, murder, and adultery referenced by James are all Old Testament commandments.)

331   Jesus declared that anyone who follows all the commandments based on Leviticus 19:18 will inherit life in the age to come (Matthew 19:16-19). Paul declared that anyone who loves others has fulfilled the Law because only the commandments based on Leviticus 19:18 are the Law (Romans 13:8-9). James declared Leviticus 19:18 to be the Messianic King's Law (James 2:8 original Greek), then listed three Old Testament commandments based on Leviticus 19:18 (2:9-11), then said that all humanity will be judged according to that Law (2:12). James concluded by saying that anyone who fulfills that Law by showing compassion will triumph on judgment day (2:13). In all three teachings from Jesus, Paul, and James, Leviticus 19:18 was the entirety of the religious legal obligation.

Epilogue

The ancient Jewish people divided their law into two groups of commandments demarcated by Leviticus 19:18. The Justices of the Torah were all the legal commandments based on "Love your neighbor as yourself." The Jobs of the Torah were all the legal commandments not based on Leviticus 19:18. Meanwhile, they were also waiting for a prophesied ruler—the Messianic King—to come and teach God's true Law. Jesus claimed to be the Messianic King and he declared that only the Justices were the Law.

Paul from Tarsus was infuriated by those who followed Jesus' teaching. He was zealous for the Jobs, even more so than most of his contemporaries. So he persecuted the Christians to the death. Meanwhile, Paul was racked with guilt over his inability to stop coveting. In fact, the more he tried to stop trespassing against this Justice of the Torah, the more he ended up violating it. He was consumed by coveting and found that his knowledge of the Law only seemed to increase his coveting all the more.

One day, Paul encountered Jesus and everything changed. He received the Spirit by faith and the Spirit wrote Leviticus 19:18 upon his heart. His previous sins were forgiven and he was empowered to no longer covet but practice altruism instead. For in accordance with a Jewish prophecy regarding the Messianic Age, the Spirit had come and written God's Law upon his heart.

Paul went forth to teach others about the Law of the Messianic King. He taught them that Leviticus 19:18 is the entire Law and that anyone can live up to God's standard by receiving the Spirit through faith in Jesus.

Paul was very careful to uphold the Law of the Messianic King in everything he taught. When it came to idolatry, he handled idolatrous practices that violate Leviticus 19:18 very differently than he handled practices that do not. He did the same with sex and sexuality. Taking another man's woman and raping young boys were mortal sins. Pre-marital sex with prostitutes and cultic, idolatrous, homosexual orgy fests were not mortal sin. Paul was careful to toe the line on everything, including jealousy, strife, anger, drunkenness, and even his discussions on salvation itself.

Gentile Christianity was unaware of the Jewish division of the law. It's unawareness of the Justices and the Jobs caused the first three chapters of Romans to remain a mystery for 2,000 years. Unawareness of the Justices and Jobs also caused Christianity to miss the very core of Paul's theology; namely that the Law of the Messianic King is the precept, "Love your neighbor as yourself."

Today, Christianity continues to misunderstand the historical Paul, and its misunderstanding is being broadcast to the world through its fierce condemnation of homosexuals. In a sad twist of irony, modern Christians invoke Paul's name to promote their anti-homosexual ideology. But Paul's stance on homosexuality isn't a theological issue; it's a historical one. Historically speaking, the Jewish prohibition against homosexuality was a Job of the Torah. Historically speaking, the apostle Paul wrote that Christians are not under the Jobs, only the Justices. He even went so far as to condemn Christians who promoted even one Job of the Torah. From a historical perspective, it is *impossible* for Paul to have considered homosexuality, a Job of the Torah, to be an impediment to entering the kingdom of God.

There is no doubt that the historical Paul would be appalled that his writings have been changed to promote the need to keep any Job of the Torah, including the ancient prohibition on homosexuality. Paul gave his life's blood to teach that only the Justices matter. However, it has taken 2,000 years for his original message to finally be revealed. But now that the 2,000-year mystery has been definitively solved, it's time for Christianity to adjust its doctrines to match what the historical Paul actually taught.

It's time for Christianity to embrace the full acceptance of homosexuals who love their neighbors as themselves. It's time for the Church to demonstrate its testimony of Jesus by being on the front line of the fight for full equality of gays and lesbians, without exception. It's time for the Church to advertise on television, on radio—even in airplane-writing in the sky, if necessary—that any youngster who is bullied in school or rejected in their family has a place of unconditional love to turn to. It is time for the Church to teach its youth to band together to stand up to school bullies, to save the precious lives of their fellow classmates. Wouldn't it be wonderful if churches taught their youth how to stand up for their fellow human beings at an early age? That would be a great and visible testimony for Jesus of Nazareth and his apostle Paul. What a wonderful world that would be…

Excerpt from

Breaking the Romans Code

Chapter 2

Insufficient Inputs

In this book, we're going to use a revolutionary new method to understand the Bible: Biblical Cryptanalysis. Now, if you are skeptical that any new approach can yield historic results, I acknowledge and respect your reservations. After all, how can a new method uncover anything remarkable about the most analyzed text on the planet? Actually, there's a straightforward cryptographic answer to that question.

All codes, even the easiest ones, require a sufficient number of inputs before they can be solved. If a cryptographer is handed the most simplistic child's code and only a small number of input/output pairs, he still won't be able to determine the key until he has more inputs. Biblical scholars have been in a similar situation with Jesus' teachings for fifteen hundred years. Even though tremendously gifted scholars existed during these times, they've been operating off a limited number of inputs—too few to find the key. Mostly, they were missing information regarding first century Jewish culture and Law.

For example, consider the ancient Jewish idiom "to have an evil eye." Today's English meaning for "evil eye" is extremely different from the ancient Jewish one. In first century Judea to "have an evil eye" meant "to be stingy" and "to have a good eye" meant "to be generous." The idiom was based on eyeing material things over the needs of others.

Those with a bad eye focus on the material things.[332, 333, 334] Those with a good eye focus on the needs of others.

With this in mind, let's take a look at how the seventeenth century King James Bible translated a sentence from Jesus' Sermon on the Mount.

> If thine eye be evil, thy whole body shall be full of darkness.[335]

The King James translation was the official Bible for almost three hundred years. So for three hundred years, Christians believed that Jesus warned against having an 'evil eye.' For three centuries, they didn't know that he was actually warning against being stingy—a different message altogether.

Before the King James Bible, the Latin Vulgate was the official Bible for almost thirteen hundred years. So how well did it do with this Hebraism?

> But if thy eye be evil thy whole body shall be darksome.[336]

Not well. The Latin Vulgate didn't grasp the idiom either. So between the Latin Vulgate and the King James Bible, Christians were told for fifteen hundred years that Jesus warned them not to fill their bodies with darkness by having an evil eye. For fifteen hundred years, Christians didn't know what Jesus actually taught:

> If your eye stingily focuses on material things, your whole body will be full of darkness.

John Calvin's writings show us how unaware the Protestant Reformers were regarding Jewish idioms. When Calvin commented on the "evil eye", he wrote:

---

332 *A Commentary on the Gospel of Matthew* by Craig S. Keener (Jul 1999) p. 232. (Craig S. Keener (PhD, Duke University) is professor of Biblical studies at Palmer Theological Seminary of Eastern University.)
333 *Eerdmans Dictionary of the Bible* by David Noel Freedman, Allen C. Myers, Astrid B. Beck, p. 498
334 *Dictionary of Jesus and the Gospels* (The IVP Bible Dictionary Series) by Joel B. Green, Scot McKnight, and I. Howard Marshall p. 472. (Joel B. Green is Dean of Academic Affairs at Asbury Theological Seminary and Professor of New Testament Interpretation.)
335 Matthew 6:23 KJV
336 Matthew 6:23 Latin Vulgate

An evil eye means a diseased eye ... they shut their eyes to avoid the light which was offered to them, because they are knowingly and willingly carried after their own lusts.[337]

Calvin wrote authoritatively. Calvin wrote charismatically. Calvin wrote with conviction. And yet, Calvin was wrong. Again, it's not his fault. He wrote in an information vacuum and did the best he could. But unfortunately, one error begets another ... creating a negative feedback loop. By not knowing that Jesus meant 'don't be stingy,' Calvin carried forward his own erroneous concept into his interpretation of what the "darkness" meant:

darkness signifies gross and brutal affections. The meaning is, we ought not to wonder, if men wallow so disgracefully, like beasts, in the filth of vices, for they have no reason which might restrain the blind and dark lusts of the flesh.[338]

Jesus' "don't be stingy with your belongings" has now been turned into a warning against living "disgracefully, like beasts, in the filth of vices." The snowball is rolling downhill ... fast.

The 'evil eye' passage was never a diatribe against filthy vices. Rather it was one of the most humanitarian passages in the entire Bible.

Accumulate for yourselves treasures in heaven, where neither moth nor rust destroys, and where thieves do not break in or steal; for where your treasure is, there your heart will be also. The eye is the lamp of the body; so then if your eye generously focuses on the needs of others, your whole body will be full of light. But if your eye stingily focuses on material things, your whole body will be full of darkness.[339]

The passage discusses storing up treasures in heaven by generously sharing with those in need. In fact, this passage was seamlessly related to something that Jesus had taught before it:

But when you give to the poor, do not let your left hand know what your right hand is doing, so that your giving will be in secret; and your Father who sees what is done in secret will reward you.[340]

---

337   *Commentary on Matthew, Mark, Luke* by John Calvin, entry for Matthew 6:22-24
338   *Commentary on Matthew, Mark, Luke* by John Calvin, entry for Matthew 6:22-24
339   Matthew 6:19-23
340   Matthew 6:3-4 NASB

Jesus had already discussed receiving a heavenly reward for generously sharing with those in need. And his first century audience understood how the "good eye vs. evil eye" seamlessly related to it.

But what happens when a person doesn't know the meaning of the "good eye vs. evil eye"? How can he possibly see the seamless fluidity of the passage? He cannot, as John Calvin illustrates. When commenting on "the eye is the lamp of the body", Calvin wrote:

> We must bear in mind, as I have already hinted, that what we find here are detached sentences, and not a continued discourse.[341]

This sentence is quite revealing. John Calvin had "already been hinting" that the entire sermon is a mishmash of "detached sentences, and not a continued discourse." His lack of knowledge regarding Hebraisms caused him to view the entire sermon as a set of detached, standalone, disconnected teachings.

Now let's think about this for a moment. As long as scholars didn't know what the "evil eye" referred to (say, for about fifteen hundred years), it was impossible for them to look for a single unified message in the Sermon on the Mount. After all, they already 'knew' the sermon was a bunch of "detached sentences, and not a continued discourse."

But it turns out that the "evil eye" wasn't disconnected at all. In fact, it was a virtual restatement of something that Jesus had just previously taught: People store up treasures in heaven when they generously share with those in need. So is it possible that the entire sermon is a continuous discourse after all? And if it is, how can we possibly recover its original seamless fluidity? That's where Biblical cryptanalysis comes in.

---

341 *Commentary on Matthew, Mark, Luke* by John Calvin, entry for Matthew 6:22-24

Chapter 3

Biblical Code Breaking

So what does cryptanalysis (the breaking of codes) have to do with the Bible anyway? Actually, it has everything to do with the Bible. Let's take a look at how a single new input combined with cryptanalysis can produce a historic result.

Jesus' Sermon on the Mount uses the Koine Greek word *dikaiosune* three times. And the Jewish audience that he was addressing had a special Hebraic understanding of this word. The Jewish communities used this word as a synonym for the Hebrew word *chesed* which meant 'loving kindness.' This can be traced back as far as 200 B.C. when the Jewish scriptures were translated into Greek. The ancient translators used the Greek word *dikaiosune* in some passages when translating the Hebrew word *chesed*.[342]

The Jewish use of *dikaiosune* as an expression of loving kindness continued to strengthen over time. By Jesus' day, *dikaiosune* was associated with charitable deeds done for others, such as giving alms to the poor.[343] In fact, Jesus himself used the word this way in his Sermon on the Mount:

> Beware of practicing your **dikaiosune** before men to be noticed by them; otherwise you have no reward with your Father who is in heaven. So **when you give to the poor**, do not sound a trumpet before you, as the hypocrites do in the synagogues and in the streets, so that they may be honored by men truly I say to you, they have their reward in full. But **when you give to**

---

342 See Genesis 19:19, 20:13, 21:23, 24:27, 32:10 LXX
343 *Meet the Rabbis: Rabbinic Thought and the Teachings of Jesus* by Brad H. Young, pp. 9-10

the poor, do not let your left hand know what your right hand is doing,[344]

Giving alms to the poor was considered one of the highest acts of loving kindness. Notice that the passage describes this expression of loving kindness as "practicing your *dikaiosune*." Now that we understand how deeply the first century Jews equated *dikaiosune* with the kind treatment of others, we are ready to perform our first Biblical cryptanalysis.

The lengthy passage below is one of the more popular passages in the New Testament. I am going to demonstrate how one new input (*dikaiosune*) combined with cryptanalysis can result in a historic Biblical finding—the recovery of an essential teaching of Jesus', which had remained unknown for fifteen hundred years.

> For I say to you that unless your ***dikaiosune*** surpasses that of the scribes and Pharisees, you will not enter the kingdom of heaven.
>
> You have heard that the ancients were told, 'YOU SHALL NOT COMMIT MURDER' and 'Whoever commits murder shall be liable to the court.' But I say to you that everyone who is angry with his brother shall be guilty before the court; and whoever says to his brother, 'You good-for-nothing,' shall be guilty before the supreme court; and whoever says, 'You fool,' shall be guilty enough to go into the fiery hell.
>
> Therefore if you are presenting your offering at the altar, and there remember that your brother has something against you, leave your offering there before the altar and go; first be reconciled to your brother, and then come and present your offering. Make friends quickly with your opponent at law while you are with him on the way, so that your opponent may not hand you over to the judge, and the judge to the officer, and you be thrown into prison. Truly I say to you, you will not come out of there until you have paid up the last cent.
>
> You have heard that it was said, 'YOU SHALL NOT COMMIT ADULTERY'; but I say to you that everyone who looks at a woman with lust for her has already committed adultery with her in his heart. If your right eye makes you stumble, tear it out and throw it from you; for it is better for you to lose one of the parts of your body, than for your whole body to be thrown into hell. If your right hand makes you stumble, cut it off and throw it from you; for it is better for you to lose one of the parts of your body, than for your whole body to go into hell.

---

344   Matthew 6:1-3 NASB with *dikaiosune* left untranslated

It was said, 'WHOEVER SENDS HIS WIFE AWAY, LET HIM GIVE HER A CERTIFICATE OF DIVORCE'; but I say to you that everyone who divorces his wife, except for the reason of unchastity, makes her commit adultery; and whoever marries a divorced woman commits adultery.

Again, you have heard that the ancients were told, 'YOU SHALL NOT MAKE FALSE VOWS, BUT SHALL FULFILL YOUR VOWS TO THE LORD.' But I say to you, make no oath at all, either by heaven, for it is the throne of God, or by the earth, for it is the footstool of His feet, or by Jerusalem, for it is THE CITY OF THE GREAT KING. Nor shall you make an oath by your head, for you cannot make one hair white or black. But let your statement be, 'Yes, yes' or 'No, no'; anything beyond these is of evil.

You have heard that it was said, 'AN EYE FOR AN EYE, AND A TOOTH FOR A TOOTH.' But I say to you, do not resist an evil person; but whoever slaps you on your right cheek, turn the other to him also. If anyone wants to sue you and take your shirt, let him have your coat also. Whoever forces you to go one mile, go with him two. Give to him who asks of you, and do not turn away from him who wants to borrow from you.

You have heard that it was said, 'YOU SHALL LOVE YOUR NEIGHBOR and hate your enemy.' But I say to you, love your enemies and pray for those who persecute you, so that you may be sons of your Father who is in heaven; for He causes His sun to rise on the evil and the good, and sends rain on the righteous and the unrighteous. For if you love those who love you, what reward do you have? Do not even the tax collectors do the same? If you greet only your brothers, what more are you doing than others? Do not even the Gentiles do the same? Therefore you are to be perfect, as your heavenly Father is perfect.[345]

Before I reveal my cryptanalysis of this passage, let's take a look at what the first sentence means. The first sentence says:

Unless your *dikaiosune* is greater than the religious leaders you cannot enter the kingdom of heaven.

And from our knowledge of the *dikaiosune* Hebraism, we know this sentence means:

Unless you treat people better than the religious leaders you cannot enter the kingdom of heaven.

By combining just one new input (*dikiosune*) with Biblical cryptanalysis, we recover the lost meaning of the passage:

345   Matthew 5:20-48 NASB with *dikaiosune* left untranslated.

- You have heard 'don't murder' and 'those who murder shall be liable to the court.'

  o **But I tell you that you have to treat people better than that.** Anyone who is angry with his brother is liable to the court and anyone who calls his brother a name is in danger of hellfire.

- You have heard 'don't commit adultery.'

  o **But I tell you that you have to treat people better than that.** Don't ogle a woman lustfully with your eyes or you're already an adulterer. It would be better for you to have no eyes if you can't stop offending your wife and the woman you are ogling.

- It was said that anyone can divorce his wife simply by giving her a certificate of divorce.

  o **But I tell you that you have to treat people better than that.** You can only divorce a woman if she's been unfaithful to you. And anyone who marries the divorced unfaithful woman shares in her adultery.

- You have heard the ancients were told not to make false vows, but to fulfill vows to the Lord.

  o **But I tell you that you have to treat people better than that.** Just keep your word even without oaths. Let your 'yes' be 'yes' and your 'no' be 'no'. Period.

- You have heard 'an eye for an eye, and a tooth for a tooth.'

  o **But I tell you that you have to treat people better than that.** Don't take revenge on a person who injures you. Offer him assistance instead. You have heard that you should love your countrymen and hate your enemies.

  o **But I tell you that you have to treat people better than that.** You need to love your enemies and pray for those who harm you. Otherwise you will not reap the reward.

Now think about what Biblical cryptanalysis has already done. We've unified twenty-nine sentences via a single statement, and we've uncovered the lost meaning of the passage as a result. The passage had always been describing how a first century Jew could treat his neighbor better than what his religion taught; nothing more, nothing less. This opens up an entirely new understanding about Jesus and his message.

Let's take divorce as an example. In the first century, many religious leaders allowed a man to divorce his wife if he found her displeasing in any way.[346] Women were sent away at the whim of their husbands. Jesus wanted the husbands to treat their wives better than that. *That's* why Jesus implemented his rule. He also didn't want women to use his unfaithfulness clause to break their marriage to be with another man. He wanted the wife to treat her husband better than that. So he said that all women who are divorced under his standard of adultery can't remarry.

The motivation behind all the rules was to get his followers to start treating *everyone* better … even women … even foreign enemies. It's actually a beautiful passage once the code has been cracked.

---

346 *Meet the Rabbis: Rabbinic Thought and the Teachings of Jesus* by Brad H. Young, p. 41

Chapter 4
The Key

In cryptography, we know that we've found the key to a code when the following happens:

All known inputs + Key = Intelligible output

When all the inputs combined with the key result in intelligible output, we know we are done... we know that we have found the key. In the last chapter, we found a single statement which accounted for all twenty-nine sentences (all twenty-nine inputs). And when we combined all twenty-nine inputs with that singular statement, we got a magnified level of intelligible output. So we're done (with that passage). We've found the key.

But think what this means. For fifteen hundred years, no one knew what Jesus had actually taught: Unless you treat people better than the religious leaders, you cannot enter the kingdom of heaven. No one knew this particular passage taught that love of neighbor is the prerequisite to entering the kingdom of heaven. No one knew that all twenty-nine sentences contributed together to convey this one singular message.

So research into first century Jewish culture combined with old fashioned cryptanalysis yielded a historic result—and this is just one teaching. Imagine what we might discover if we found the key to the entire Sermon on the Mount! If we could find a single statement that accounts for the sermon from beginning to end, then perhaps we'll discover that the entire sermon is very different from what Christians thought for fifteen hundred years.

What if we sought to find the key to all of Jesus' teachings on salvation and judgment in the Gospel of Matthew?   Would we find that Jesus' salvation teachings were different than what Christians have thought for fifteen hundred years?

What about Paul's letter to the Romans: Is it even possible to find a single statement that encompasses every sentence in this lengthy letter from beginning to end? And if we did, would we find that the Biblical book that modern Christianity is based upon actually teaches something different than what Christians thought for fifteen hundred years?

Armed with new knowledge regarding first century culture and law, we have sufficient inputs to finally solve these three massive puzzles:

Puzzle #1:   The Sermon on the Mount

Puzzle #2:   The Gospel of Matthew

Puzzle #3:   Romans

As you will soon see, a whole host of Biblical surprises reveal themselves at every twist and turn in solving these puzzles. Christianity is about to discover that the most essential teaching (The Sermon on the Mount) and the most essential Biblical books (Matthew and Romans) are extremely different from what Christians believed for fifteen hundred years. And Biblical cryptanalysis is going to prove it.

[Chapters 5-6 are not included in this excerpt.]

Chapter 7

The Body Eclectic

The body of the Sermon on the Mount is comprised of the following seven teachings:

**The Body of Jesus'
Sermon on the Mount**

1. Only if you treat people better than the scribes and the Pharisees can you enter the kingdom of heaven. (Matthew 5:20-48)

2. Your Father in heaven will reward you when you secretly give to the poor. (Matthew 6:1-4)

3. God will forgive your sins in direct proportion to your forgiveness of others. (Matthew 6:5-15)

4. You store up treasures in heaven by generously sharing with those in need. (Matthew 6:19-24)

5. Don't worry about your own needs. Just focus on bringing God's kingdom to earth by expressing loving kindness[347] and God will meet your needs as well. (Matthew 6:25-34)

6. Whatever measure you use on others, God will use on you. (Matthew 7:1-6)

---

347 This teaching uses the Hebraic idiom *dikaiosune*, which referred to expressing loving kindness. See Chapter 3, "Biblical Code Breaking," for details.

7. Treat others well, because as a child of God,[348] your heavenly Father will give you far greater rewards than you can possibly give even to your own family. (Matthew 7:7-11)

Now that we've organized the sermon into a manageable structure, we're ready to find the key. We're ready to find a single statement that accounts for all seven teachings (and thereby, every sentence between the introduction and the surprising conclusion).

The cryptanalytic answer is given below:

The Key to the Body of Jesus' Sermon on the Mount

1. **God is going to treat you based on how you treat others.** Therefore, only if you treat people better than the scribes and the Pharisees can you enter the kingdom of heaven. (Matthew 5:20-48)

2. **God is going to treat you based on how you treat others.** Therefore, your Father in heaven will reward you when you secretly give to the poor. (Matthew 6:1-4)

3. **God is going to treat you based on how you treat others.** Therefore, God will forgive your sins in direct proportion to your forgiveness of others. (Matthew 6:5-15)

4. **God is going to treat you based on how you treat others.** Therefore, you store up treasures in heaven by generously sharing with those in need. (Matthew 6:19-24)

5. **God is going to treat you based on how you treat others.** Therefore, don't worry about your own needs. Just focus on bringing God's kingdom to earth by expressing loving kindness[349] and God will meet your needs as well. (Matthew 6:25-34)

6. **God is going to treat you based on how you treat others.** Therefore, whatever measure you use on others, God will use on you. (Matthew 7:1-6)

---

348 Jesus already stated in Matthew 5:44-45 that only those who love others are children of the heavenly Father. This is the prerequisite for being in the adoptive position of receiving gifts from the heavenly Father.

349 This teaching uses the Hebraic idiom *dikaiosune* which referred to expressing loving kindness. See Chapter 3, "Biblical Code Breaking," for details.

7. **God is going to treat you based on how you treat others.** Therefore, treat others well, because as a child of God,[350] your heavenly Father will give you far greater rewards than you can possibly give even to your own family. (Matthew 7:7-11)

Jesus used the body of the sermon to repeat a single principle seven times over: *God is going to treat you based on how you treat others.* The teachings of the body provide the theological basis for the conclusion:

- *Introduction* - I promise to give an interpretation of the Law and the Prophets that preserves every commandment down to the smallest one.

- *Body* - God is going to treat you based on the way you treat others.

- *Conclusion* - Therefore, treating others the same way that you want to be treated is the entire Law and the Prophets.

Now we can see why insufficient inputs made finding the key impossible for so many centuries. How could scholars find the key when they had to put 'don't have an evil eye which neglects guidance of affections' into the mix? How could scholars find the key when they had to include 'don't wallow so disgracefully, like beasts, in the filth of vices?' It was impossible for scholars to find the key for many centuries. They had insufficient inputs.

The insufficient inputs created a negative feedback loop, causing them to conclude that Jesus' sermon was a discontinuous set of free-floating ideas and instructions.[351] Therefore, they didn't even look for a key which could encompass it all, for they had already concluded that such a thing couldn't possibly exist.

But now, everything's changed. We finally have enough inputs to solve the entire puzzle. How do we know that we have enough inputs? Let me ask you a question: When you bring home a puzzle, how do you know when you've solved it? Simple, once the assembly

---

350 Jesus already stated in Matthew 5:44-45 that only those who love others are children of the heavenly Father. This is the prerequisite for being in the adoptive position of receiving gifts from the heavenly Father.

351 John Calvin wrote that he considered the sermon as a whole to be a conglomeration of "detached sentences, and not a continued discourse." See Commentary on *Matthew, Mark, Luke* by John Calvin, entry for Matthew 6:22-24.

contains all the pieces, you know that you've solved the puzzle. You know you are done. Likewise, the moment our assembly of the Sermon on the Mount contains all the pieces, we know that we are done.

[End of Excerpt]

CPSIA information can be obtained
at www.ICGtesting.com
Printed in the USA
BVHW080919140720
583601BV00004B/537